# What readers

"The science is in. In this book, Ines sets out the new path for businesses to follow to create workplaces of our future. Anyone reading this can go and create real, sustainable change in their teams and organisations for better straight away."

*Sarah Metcalfe, Chief Happiness Officer & Co-Leader, Woohoo Unlimited*

"This book will challenge you to combine collaboration, sustainability and emotional intelligence to create a better business. Ines' experience in innovation makes her the perfect author to explore how thinking beyond profit alone can lead to more impact."

*Meggie Palmer, Founder PepTalkHer, Fortune 500 Executive Coach & Facilitator*

"Millions of years of evolution of nature have given the human being with its intelligence. Adopting in society in general and in the business world in particular simply, or even exclusively, the principles of the "law of the jungle" or the "law of the strongest" is an unacceptable waste. Ines Garcia's book provides us with references and cases in which the admirable potential of human intelligence is applied to business in search of an economic development that is environmentally responsible and, above all, socially inclusive. It is a complex but mandatory path, full of challenges and in which, at the moment, we are all apprentices. Hence the importance of this work to help the fundamental efforts to achieve a sustainable happy profit."

*Wagner de Siqueira Pinto, ESG, Sustainability, Corporate Social Responsibility Advisor*

# Sustainable Happy Profit

## Products and Organisations that Thrive

# Also by Ines Garcia

Becoming more Agile whilst delivering Salesforce

Better Estimates

# Sustainable Happy Profit

## Products and Organisations that Thrive

by Ines Garcia

Sustainable Happy Profit
Products and Organisations that Thrive
Ines Garcia

Published by Get Agile Ltd
A record for this book is available from the British Library.

Ebook ISBN: 978-1-8381631-3-6
Print ISBN: 978-1-8381631-2-9

*Amazon Print-On-Demand is Forest Stewardship Council-certified on their printing practices for paperback books, more: tiny.cc/amazonprint. We all should be working to do our part to protect the environment.*

*This book can be purchased only digitally or by 'print-on-demand'. Only and only when a book is purchased in physical format does it go into a queue to be printed; as unfortunately most of the high street books today sadly end up in landfill. Here is our effort to reduce waste and carbon footprint.*

*To you,*
*and the legacy we leave behind.*

# Contents

# A note from the author

Sustainable. Happy. Profit.

I bet you hear and use these words on a daily basis, often more than once a day. They're simple words, with complex connotations.

Being **sustainable** is not just about the product itself which is built to endure over time. It's also about the people, time and energy involved in the process, and the consumption that its existence requires. If any single part of the process cannot be maintained over time, it's unsustainable.

Intrinsically, we humans want to be **happy**. I'm talking about evaluative happiness, rather than affective happiness (which is how one feels right now or in the recent past). Evaluative happiness tends to be more stable, and therefore sustainable. Happiness derives from having a purpose, i.e. the pursuit of an interesting and challenging *something*, which is greater than oneself. As humans, we are naturally driven to contribute and challenge ourselves.

Three key factors to enable better business performance are speed, stability and the availability of our products and services. And performance directly impacts **profit**, productivity and customer satisfaction. Afterall a company needs to remain commercially viable and, whilst we can't forget our finances, the term profit encompasses much more than just financial gain.

As a business owner myself, these are words that mean a lot to me. They act as the foundations for the organisation, products and ecosystem that I am building towards. My aim, as with most business owners, is to build something that achieves more than traditional economic growth.

Ines Garcia, 2021

# Introduction

When we think about growth within our organisations we can correlate it to socio-economics for a macro view of the overarching system perspective.

It has taken quite some time, and now there seems to be a common understanding that Gross Domestic Product (GDP) as an indicator of economic health is, in fact, not a good indicator of a healthy standard of living at all. It does not account for leisure, environmental quality, levels of health and education, changes in inequality, increases in variety, fluctuation in technology, the value that society may place on certain outputs, or indeed any of the activities external to market value.

Unfortunately for all of us, economics over the past 80 years has been obsessed with GDP as the primary measure of progress. However, now we know (as many have been seeing and saying for a while) that it's not just a bad metric, it also has detrimental repercussions.

Recent IPCC reports warn us that economic models are ineffective at capturing the full range of impacts.[1] For example, although climate action produces significant 'co-benefits'—

1        IPCC, *AR5 Climate Change 2014: Impacts, Adaptation, and Vulnerability,* http://www.ipcc.ch/report/ar5/wg2

such as reducing air pollution that contributes to around 3.7 million deaths each year—this is not represented in any mitigation costs analysis.

Individuals in any organisation—especially CEOs, CFOs, CTOs, VPs, Heads of Department, Team Leads, you name it—need to see beyond their *wallets* and use a better measure of progress. Growth is not an endless entity, it can't be. So, by only basing our strategy, time and efforts on Profit and Loss (PnL), we're missing most of the picture.

Better measures of progress are at our disposal, we need to create a new narrative and a shared vision to draw a future that is sustainable, that illustrates the full picture, and that's in balance with our environment.

As a business owner, balancing all three of these big variables, without any compromise, may seem like a mammoth task. No doubt, it's a job with huge uncertainties, and a lot of big questions to ask. Where do we even start? What do we want to change? What outcome should we be aiming for? How aware are we of the currently diminishing state of each and every one of our businesses? You are not alone. I was just as unsure myself, and that's why I began this quest.

The Sustainable Development Goals, that will be discussed further, have been a powerful agreement achieved by governments and businesses around the world. They outline best practices for organisations to adopt, to help to create a healthier environment as a whole. However, what must be recognised is the additional impact resulting from what other organisations are doing right now to move towards a sustainable world, and how specifically they are doing it.

Why should we care?

> *"Economics is, at root, the study of incentives: how people get what they want, or need, especially when other people want or need the same thing. (...) An incentive is simply a means of urging people to do more of a good thing and less of a bad thing."[2]*

Steven D. Levitt and Stephen J. Dubner

Firstly, I'll drop some macro-incentives here:

The health of nature is intimately linked to the health of humans. The emergence of new infectious diseases tends to be related to the destruction of forests and wilderness. Healthy ecosystems are the foundation of today's global economies and societies, and the ones we aspire to build. As more and more species are drawn towards extinction, the very life support systems which civilisation depends on are dissolving.

Of the nine greatest threats to the world, as ranked by the World Economic Forum organisation,[3] six relate to the ongoing destruction of nature. The degradation of our ecosystem has an impact on agricultural output, food prices and levels of poverty. It equally has a ripple effect on employment as people who work in the tourism and travel industry could see their incomes fall over the long-run.

Resolving that is not only down to conservation areas and governmental policies; it's also down to shifting to more sustainable methods of production and consumption. And it's there where we can make a dent.

You may have heard of Green Recovery. This is a widely adopted name for a set of reforms aiming to recover prosperity after the COVID-19 pandemic. Changes of whatever nature,

---

2    Steven D. Levitt and Stephen J. Dubner, *Freakonomics: A Rogue Economist Explores the Hidden Side of Everything* (New York: HarperCollins, 2020)

3    World Economic Forum, *The Global Risks Report 2020,* www3.weforum.org/docs/WEF_Global_Risk_Report_2020.pdf

open a window of opportunity. We have experienced direct short-term positive impacts from reduced human activity, ranging from reduction of greenhouse gas (GHG) emissions and energy consumption to air quality and noise pollution. Green Recovery focuses on improving operations, reducing carbon emissions, creating green jobs, expanding renewable energy sources, etc., so it accounts for future environment and climate justice for the planet, and the livelihoods of everyone on it. Change is opportunity and, as with any opportunity, you either grab it or miss it.

In traditional economic studies, how energy drives economic and social activity is barely noted. We can't continue to dismiss the role that the flow of energy plays in the flow of income and of being.

> *"We are embedded in the living world, not separate from or above it: we live within the biosphere, not on the planet."*[4]

Kate Raworth

We are facing a new energy transition. In terms of technology, the challenge of our century is moving from fossil fuel to clean energy sources, and to generate smart electricity grids. The challenge is not about if we will make the shift, but if we will make it in time. This transition involves changing the paradigm by looking at it from another angle, a cultural change has to be undertaken as well. We need to be mindful that we don't simply swap fuel-dependency for material-intensity. Electric vehicles, energy storage systems and the extension of electricity grids need finite materials such as lithium, cobalt,

---

4        Kate Raworth, *Doughnut Economics: Seven Ways to Think Like a 21st-Century Economist* (New York: Random House, 2018)

nickel, copper, zinc, silicon and rare earth materials, as the IEA points out.[5]

Take the *circular economy* concept as an example related to energy and material efficiency. A circular economy is an alternative to the *linear economy* that we are just so used to (Take-Make-Waste). In a circular economy we keep resources in use for as long as possible, maximising their value with recovery and regeneration of products, materials and energy at heart. Eco-design is especially important here, because 80% of the sustainability-specific decisions surrounding a new product are made during the design and development stages. So a materials science approach can significantly reduce the environmental impact that new products are responsible for. Circular economy is also related to the life-cycle assessments, which we'll cover later on.

Focusing on renewable sources is generally the largest, cheapest, most benign and most quickly deployable way to provide energy services. Yet it is also the least visible, least understood and least addressed. Its positive impact is comparable to the change itself: energy efficiency makes its supply cheaper. In addition, this brings a reinforcing benefit, especially when combined with onsite renewable supplies, making them nonlinearly smaller, simpler, and cheaper. Win, win, win.

One big problem we have in the energy transition arena is that it's probably the one contributing to excessive pollution, but we do not get feedback on the environmental consequences of our day-to-day actions. For example if your company's use of energy produces air pollution, you are unlikely to know or appreciate that fact, certainly not on a continual basis. Even if you know about the connection, it's probably not salient to your behaviour.

---

5        IEA, *The Role of Critical Minerals in Clean Energy Transitions,*        www.iea.org/reports/the-role-of-critical-miner-als-in-clean-energy-transitions

Luckily, several local governments and companies are undertaking both technological and cultural transformations, geared towards sustainable practices, systems and goals. These aim to build a better place to live, by doing things now, for the benefit of future generations.

The importance lies in seeking for diverse teams, fostering and building upon each other's perspectives and enriching ideas. To build resilient, inclusive and competitive organisations, for better products, communities and impacts. Currently, in our ever-changing and fast-paced world, our organisations have become stagnant. This goes beyond our own individual boundaries, as what we do has an impact on the environment we are part of.

I'm inviting you to be part of the solution.

Each organisation faces pressure from all angles to implement decarbonisation strategies which have never been stronger, a report from KPMG and Eversheds Sutherland finds. Investors, key influencers, regulators, and employees have turned the spotlight on climate issues, and now an "ever-increasing size of the consumer demographic that has put climate change at the top of their priorities cannot be ignored".[6]

Observing the efforts from governments globally, we can see that their plans are too slow and clunky for what is needed. Back in 2015, the Paris Climate Conference took place. Countries around the world signed agreements to combat climate change. In my view, those have failed. Most countries have not hit the goals they committed to.[7] We can't wait for laws and policies that invite failure, we need to be more agile.

---

6       Eversheds Sutherland and KPMG IMPACT, *Climate change and corporate value,* https://assets.kpmg/content/dam/kpmg/xx/pdf/2021/03/climate-change-and-corporate-value.pdf

7       The Climate Action Tracker is an independent scientific analysis that tracks government climate action and measures it against the globally agreed Paris Agreement aim of holding warming well below 2°C. www.climateactiontracker.org

Policies and laws are not fast enough and have loopholes. As an example, back in October 2020 a new driving law in the UK finally made it illegal to take pictures while driving. Why? When the use of phones was initially forbidden in 2010 the devices did not have photography capability. Yes, it took more than 10 years. Mad.

If we apply the same logic to environmental policies, you can see that the UK has set net-zero emissions for 2050, but continues to provide subsidies to fossil fuel companies.[8] Even as these companies are aware of the environmental damage they cause to the environment, policy incentives have been slow to respond.

We can observe the recent efforts to raise environmental awareness amongst the masses ... the individual consumer. How Sir David Attenborough's lifetime service has made our population aware of the irreversible facts from our behaviours. How Greta Thunberg, the then 15-year-old who skipped school, showed a mirror to the world, revealing the devastating threats to our livelihoods.

Aside from these two angles—politics and population—I see the biggest target gap that needs to be addressed today: YOU. So here we are. Organisations are the target audience for this book. By focusing on organisations and their contributions towards sustainability, all of us can make a big difference to making the world a better place. Being better off than the current (most often oblivious) spiral of self-destruction that organisations are in now.

In this process of evolution, we must acknowledge that we, humans, are wired to grab immediate rewards, rather than

---

8          Henri Kouam, *Environmentally dangerous fossil-fuel subsidies are also economically counterproductive!,* Medium, https://medium.datadriveninvestor.com/environmentally-dangerous-fossil-fuel-subsidies-are-also-economically-counterproductive-c69a93c72b43

those further future ones —even when it's in our interest to choose the latter. And this is why this book is needed. We must fight for a better future, even though we may not be here to see it all.

This is where Sustainable Happy Profit comes in. You do not have to wait to get those rewards, to get those results, as we focus on micro incentives.

You are holding, and about to unfold, a book focused on helping organisations of all sizes to understand what can be done, starting today, and how to (for the long term) deliver sustainable, happy and profitable products.

How can we move from intellectual nourishment and theoretical agreement to a real plan of action? We can do this by being inspired from what others are doing, which helps to depict what the new lens of Sustainable Happy Profit can mean for your organisation.

I have sectioned this book into three parts: Sustainable Happy Profit. In Part One we explore the extent of what **sustainable** means, creating a set of boundaries for our system redefinition. Part Two discusses the meaning of **happy**; whilst its definition at individual level can vary there are common components that define an environment where one can thrive. We end with Part Three by describing how **profit** becomes a tangible result.

Each one of the parts contains its own ABCs of the rudiments of the subject at hand, accompanied by organisation stories that I have learned from. In addition each of the three parts also contains a CBA, an actionable summary that you can kick start today for your Sustainable Happy Profit journey. My aim with this format of ABCs and CBAs is that through studies and real-life organisation performance analytics, we can dissect and define tangible actions that you can implement in your own environment.

Your journey starts now.

# Part One

# Sustainable

*"Ecosystems, species, wild populations, local varieties and breeds of domesticated plants and animals are shrinking, deteriorating or vanishing. The essential, interconnected web of life on Earth is getting smaller and increasingly frayed...This loss is a direct result of human activity and constitutes a direct threat to human well-being in all regions of the world."*[9]

Prof. Josef Settele

The figures speak for themselves—1 million species are threatened with extinction—and we are the reason for it. Being a part of society, we share a common responsibility for humanity's footprint, and the impact we have on our environment. Nature is not an endless source.

As leaders within our organisations, we must set clear and tangible goals to track and reduce the rate of destruction of our planet. To protect both the environment and our own businesses, and work towards becoming sustainable.

Better sustainability credentials not only allow us to maximise commercial opportunities (sales and operations) they also enhance our brands, engage stakeholders and shareholders, and

9        UN Nature Report, *Nature's Dangerous Decline 'Un-precedented'; Species Extinction Rates 'Accelerating'*, UN, www.un-.org/sustainabledevelopment/blog/2019/05/nature-decline-un-precedented-report

make our businesses better places to be involved with. And this is even without delving into the impact it will have on the not-so-far-future generations.

The rate of extinction is accelerating; this includes species, populations, plants and animals. It has a detrimental effect on every nation's health, a country's development (including its ability to grow, learn and mature), and our global climate. We must bend the curve before it's irreversible.

We can't leave the future of our planet solely in the hands of governments and policies. There is just no time, and after all, it is in our own interest to take control.

> *"We've already lost nearly 90% of the wetlands around the world. We've transformed the forests and grasslands, we've converted 75% of the land that is not covered by ice."*[10]

David Attenborough

You may be thinking sustainability extends beyond nature and yes, it does! John Fullerton identifies eight interconnected principles in his work on Regenerative Civilization,[11] from the relationship that the economy has with the environment to the understanding that wealth is not just "money in the bank". He explains the need to constantly inspect and adapt in our ever-changing environment and how this is coupled with "the quality of empowered participation" in the larger whole. He explores the credits and merits of community and place and how that translates to distributed organisations; how even

---

10      David Attenborough, *Transcript of David Attenborough's 'Extinction: The Facts'*, BBC One (13/9/2020), www.isthebbc-biased.blogspot.com/2020/09/transcript-of-david-attenboroughs.html

11      John Fullerton, *8 Principles for a Regenerative Civiliza-tion*, Films For Action, www.filmsforaction.org/articles/regenera-tive-economies-for-a-regenerative-civilization

large global corporations can foster creativity, innovation, flow and other variables as metrics beyond GDP, in striving for a balance which requires companies to "harmonize multiple variables instead of optimizing single ones."

Sustainable Development Goals have been a powerful agreement achieved by governments and businesses to adopt best practices of creating a healthy environment as a whole. The 17 Sustainable Development Goals were born at the United Nations Conference on Sustainable Development in Rio de Janeiro in 2012 with the objective to produce a set of universal goals that meet the urgent environmental, political and economic challenges facing our world.[12] The 17 goals include a total of 169 targets, also known as the "2030 agenda". The goals are a universal call to action to end poverty, protect the planet and ensure that all people enjoy peace and prosperity.

All of which can be correlated to each of our own organisations. Often, the difficulty lies in translating metrics into achievable, tangible sets of actions we can take. Let's start with the ABCs of Sustainable.

---

12      UN, *Take Action for the Sustainable Development Goals,* www.un.org/sustainabledevelopment/sustainable-development-goals

# A is for Anchor

A nchor here means to 'weigh anchor', to stop moving from one initiative to another but rather to reflect and consider where you are at right now. It involves a conscious act of deep awareness.

> *"The strongest anchor is hope."*[13]

Lailah Gifty Akita

Are greenhouse gas (GHG) emissions[14] the only focus for organisations? Or are there more dimensions to consider before a company can be classed as "sustainable"?

GHG emissions are not the only issue we face, this is (simply) a standardised, worldwide unit of measurement for understanding negative environmental impacts. You can invest your efforts into achieving several Sustainable Development Goals, rather than exclusively GHG emissions. We will later unfold the stories of Ørsted and Elopak, who linked their business goals with Sustainable Development Goals.

Sustainable Development Goals coincided with another historic agreement, reached in 2015 at the Paris Climate

---

13      Lailah Gifty Akita, *Think Great: Be Great!* (Scotts Valley: CreateSpace, 2014)

14      Greenhouse gas emissions are gases released to the atmosphere as a repercussion of human activity, such as burning fossil fuels.

Conference (COP21). Together with the Sendai Framework for Disaster Risk Reduction, signed in Japan in March 2015, these agreements provide a set of common standards and achievable targets to reduce carbon emissions, manage the risks of climate change and natural disasters, and aim to build back better after a crisis. Companies that show their commitments to Sustainable Development Goals work towards being sustainable organisations by applying a holistic approach—with a focus beyond greenhouse emissions.

Now, the world is seeking to climb back down the power density ladder, from a highly concentrated usage of fossil fuels to more dispersed renewable sources.

Vaclav Smil, a globally recognised energy expert, stated that humanity has experienced three major energy transitions and is now struggling to kick off a fourth.[15] First was the mastery of fire, which allowed us to liberate energy from the sun by burning plants. Second came farming, which converted and concentrated solar energy into food, freeing people to enjoy pursuits other than just fighting for sustenance. During that second era (which ended just a few centuries ago) farm animals and larger human populations supplied energy themselves as people and animals were used as mechanical energy forces. Third came industrialisation and, with it, the rise of fossil fuels. Coal, oil, and natural gas, each in turn, rose to prominence, and energy production became the domain of machines, such as coal-fired power plants. And now the world is beginning the shift from depending on highly concentrated and finite fossil fuels for its energy to using a range of more dispersed renewable sources.

The current energy transition involves huge investments, technological developments and agile regulations to promote and ramp up clean energy sources such as solar, wind, geothermal, hydro, biomass and "a nuclear energy new wave."

---

15     Vaclav Smil, *Energy Transitions: History, Requirements, Prospects* (Santa Barbara: Praeger, 2010)

All of these have zero $CO_2$ emissions. Yet, there are still numerous factors—like capital and financing costs, construction times, operating life and environmental impacts—to be considered. Although they have zero emissions, other environmental considerations need to be taken into account, for example, the land use of solar panels, and the nuclear waste storage and weapons proliferation issues surrounding nuclear energy. Fortunately, new debates around clean energy technologies are now taking place within and amongst governments, businesses and civil society.

Reducing waste by recycling is another way to contribute to our zero carbon challenge worldwide. Afterall the value of a company's goods and services is relative to the waste it generates. Sustainability and happiness are not at the expense of profit but a means to it. Mostly, it's the younger generations who are aware of the worst-case scenarios that might occur if we don't all reuse products and materials that could be re-introduced into global supply chains, when waste reduction and recycling should be tackled at all levels.

There are many pathways. Another approach to sustainability is to adjust our methods of farming, in line with the so-called "regenerative agriculture"[16] strategy. This has the potential to absorb vast amounts of carbon emissions, through soil regeneration and diversity.

The diverse pathways that we have towards zero carbon emissions are complementary to each other. Your target is to reduce at least your current carbon emission by 50% per year from now on.

---

16      Kiss the Ground is a range of programmes designed to awaken people to a "'*new, old approach*' to farming called 'regenerative agriculture' that has the potential to balance our climate, replenish our vast water supplies, and feed the world." www.kisstheground.com

**Why are we so concerned with carbon emissions?**

Carbon is not intrinsically a bad thing—it is a crucial part of what humans are made of, as well as being key to pretty much everything else on planet earth. The issue we have with carbon is down to industrialisation and practices that over-generate it, thereby emitting high volumes of carbon into the atmosphere.

Naturally, $CO_2$ is released into the atmosphere in lots of different ways. The largest source of natural carbon emissions is from the exchange of carbon dioxide ($CO_2$) between the oceans and the atmosphere. Animals and plants also emit $CO_2$ through the process of respiration (they breathe in oxygen and breathe out $CO_2$). And, when these plants and animals decompose, organisms within the soil respire to produce energy and emit more $CO_2$ into the atmosphere.

Nature, as nature tends to do, keeps most of these emissions in balance. Plants absorb $CO_2$ through photosynthesis, and oceans absorb just about as much as they let off. Carbon cycles through our air, water and soil in a continuous process that supports life on earth.

On the other hand, when humans extract, refine, transport, and burn fossil fuels—like coal, natural gas, and oil—we release additional carbon and other GHGs into the atmosphere. We also cut down large expanses of $CO_2$-absorbing trees to make way for agriculture and new developments, or collect lumber to create new products. When these trees burn or decompose, they emit even more $CO_2$. By removing forests, we also effectively remove the natural systems that absorb and store carbon.

$CO_2$ is one of the GHGs that absorbs radiation and prevents heat from escaping our atmosphere. This excess heat creates disrupted weather patterns, higher global temperature averages and other changes in the climate, such as air pollution and its associated diseases.[17]

**So, how does one tackle the energy transition challenge?**

As I mentioned in the introduction, the challenge of our century is moving from fossil fuels to clean energy sources. A high-level global goal would be to become carbon neutral, thanks to a big shift towards renewable energies.

The energy sector is home to the world's most powerful companies, 7 of the top 10, as ranked by Global Fortune 500 in 2013. The energy sector makes up 75% of global GHG emissions. As a result, improvements in energy efficiency could reduce at least 40% of this figure.[18] The thing is that an efficient consumption of energy is everybody's responsibility, even just by themselves, the energy industry has the finance, technology and talent to be the enabler for this to happen at the scale and speed that is needed to help both individuals and corporations do this more easily and effectively.

Stop, anchor and reflect on where you are now, with awareness being the first step. Let me tell you a story:

Just 10 years ago, the Danish energy provider Ørsted was 85% fossil fuel based, and only 15% renewables based. Today, Ørsted has flipped these proportions and is now ranked the

---

17        You can access a real-time Air Pollution reading through waqi.info. Similar sources include www.iqair.com/earth and www.visuals.datadrivenlab.org/airmap_2016.

18        Alyssa Fischer, *How Energy Efficiency Will Power Net-Zero Climate Goals*, IEA (International Energy Agency), www.iea.org/commentaries/how-energy-efficiency-will-power-net-zero-climate-goals

most sustainable company in the world.[19] Providing green energy to 9.5 million people, they are set to raise this number to over 50 million people by 2030, and are employing more than 6 thousand people. The company attributes its dramatic transformation to the societal demand for green energy and aims to be carbon-neutral by 2025.

As Jakob Askou Bøss, the Senior Vice President Corporate Strategy & Stakeholder Relations of Ørsted, told me, it started from strategy analysis. They knew that, long-term, their operations which harnessed energy from fossil fuels would not be sustainable for the world, and therefore not for their own company either. By reading scientific reports about the severity of climate change they became aware there were no other options aside from changing the course and initiating a transformation to green energy. So they anchored, reflected and then changed course, with the end goal of being at the forefront of fighting climate change and developing a future business model which was sustainable, both financially and environmentally.

His personal motivation for driving this change was the realisation that until the 1970s Denmark was very dependent on other countries, mostly the Middle East, for its energy supplies. Following the oil crises in the '70s, Denmark converted the majority of its power production to coal, and developed its offshore oil and gas resources in the North Sea. This has helped the country to achieve energy independence for the past 25-30 years.

---

19      Ørsted develops, constructs and operates offshore and onshore wind farms, solar farms, energy storage facilities, and bioenergy plants, and provides energy products to its customers. Ørsted ranks #1 in Corporate Knights' 2020 index of the Global 100 most sustainable corporations and is recognised on the CDP Climate Change A List as a global leader on climate action. The business is headquartered in Denmark and in 2019 had a revenue of DKK 67.8 billion (EUR 9.1 billion).

Having undertaken that energy transition, in order to stay energy independent as a small country with a very open economy and few natural resources, Jakob believed they needed to take the lead in the renewable energy industry. This was not only to help to maintain Denmark's position as an energy independent nation—knowing how much strategic importance the energy system and supply has for a country—but also to help to accelerate the transition to a globally sustainable energy system. He is aware we face very serious challenges for planet Earth—fossil fuels being responsible for more than 70% of the global $CO_2$ emissions. As Jakob told me, "It is very motivating to give my contribution to do what I can to help address this global problem."

The inception for Ørsted started with the creation of the new brand. This brand was based on a three-way collaboration between Kontrapunkt (a leading Scandinavian design agency), Wieden and Kennedy (an international firm best known for its bold work with Nike) and an internal creative team at Danish Oil and Natural Gas (the previous brand name for Ørsted).[20] As part of the new brand, they also landed on two pieces of strategic messaging that reflected their sustainable purpose: "Love your home" as a tagline that works for both employees and consumers, and "Let's create a world that runs entirely on green energy" as a long-term mission that speaks to both consumers and investors.

We often think of investors as trying to take value away from stakeholders, when in fact investors look after funds such as retirement and pensions. Investors do much more than just hold a share (shareholder), they have an interest in the returns, they are invested and attentive to where the trade is gearing to.

---

20      Danish Oil and Natural Gas (DONG) and Ørsted are the same company (ownership and management) but Ørsted features a new business model: www.offshore-energy.biz/dong-energy-changes-name-as-it-exits-oil-and-gas-business

By investing 193 billion DKK in renewables over the last decade, and increasing the share of green energy in their energy generation to 86% by the end of 2020, Ørsted achieved an increase of profits by 28% total EBITDA[21] at the end of 2019, compared to where they were 10 years ago. One can conclude that, if you put your head, heart and efforts in the right place you can in fact make an energy source shift that has a positive impact on your bottom line.

**How to know where you stand today**

Assuming not all readers are from the energy and utilities industry, investing in solar panels for your buildings or shifting energy extraction to wind may not be the most relevant action to take today. So, what would be the best thing to do?

Your goal is to cut carbon emissions 'at source' as much as possible, and to do so the first thing we need is to anchor, and find out where each one of our organisations is at right now.

Start a life-cycle assessment to evaluate the impact of your organisation, including your value chain. You can start by identifying your processes and checking whether your raw materials could be certified as sustainable sources. Such as labels awarded by the Forest Stewardship Council, Sustainable Biomass Program (SBP), Round Table on Responsible Soy Association, COSMOS Natural standard (organic and natural cosmetics) and the European Energy Certificate System[22]. Labels like Guarantees of Origin, Renewable Energy Certificates (both for renewable electricity) and ISCC Plus for renewable polymers are examples of certifications that Elopak,

---

21     Earnings Before Interest, Taxes, Depreciation, and Amortisation (EBITDA) adds depreciation and amortisation expenses back into a company's operating profit.

22     *European Energy Certificate System*, Wikipedia, www.en.wikipedia.org/wiki/European_Energy_Certificate_System

a company we cover later on, is using. Ørsted did this life-cycle assessment exercise also to guarantee that they not only have a clean energy supply, but that they are purchasing clean inputs too.

Being aware of one's energy consumption is also an easy first step. Compare your physical consumption against your billed consumption, as you want to avoid a consumption gap between metering and bill values. Then, once you have measures and feedback, you can more proactively work towards becoming energy efficient. Even on a good old Excel file, you can analyse that data, see if you can identify peaks and troughs and ask yourself, are they avoidable in the near future?

In terms of energy, can you generate green power? Or can you switch providers? Or can you put pressure on your providers, and influence their switch to renewable energy? As an extra bonus, your energy bills most likely will be lower too.

Make an equipment inventory of things that require energy use. This will include, amongst other things cooling, hot water generation, lighting, computers and other devices. From there, identify how many devices are in your organisation, hours utilised, and the power they use. You don't have to do this manually of course, there are a lot of companies that could help you with strong data analysis software, some of which also apply machine learning to the process. In essence you want to become more aware of the following:

- Peaks and troughs in energy demand
- How to optimise space usage and consolidation
- Environmental impact of reducing waste and costs
- How to undertake plug load reduction
- Stored redundant equipment

We can learn from Ørsted that its need to change its energy generation mix from fossil fuels to renewables may have come as a long-term goal. Once it was formulated it did not entail shutting down coal-fired power plants or building new wind farms. It was a vision with a 30-year horizon, which is approximately the lifetime of their assets. And although the transformation on the subject of asset replacement is not immediate, the impact over time can be substantial.

By anchoring and taking the time to analyse your current position, you become aware of your current assets' lifetime and the system as a whole, you can take that as an opportunity and act as an enabler to make specific, conscious steps towards being sustainable. This can be implemented in every new purchase and replacement—seek products with a long shelf-life and, where possible, those which are also locally sourced and minimally packaged.

It's not just about replacing, but reusing, recovering, recycling and restoring. Landfill is the second most-used waste treatment in the UK, with 24.4% (52.3 million tonnes) of waste disposed of at landfill in 2016.[23] Whilst efforts have been made on energy recovery facilities since, the overall volume of waste sent to landfill has not shown a corresponding decrease.

---

23      Department for Environment, Food & Rural Affairs, and Government Statistical Service, *UK Statistics on Waste*, www.assets.publishing.service.gov.uk/government/uploads/system/uploads/attachment_data/file/918270/UK_Statistics_on_Waste_statistical_notice_March_2020_accessible_FINAL_updated_size_12.pdf

# B is for Become

We have only scratched the surface. From anchoring, the ability to tangibly measure where you are, and the high-level incentives reasoning, what's next? How can we become more sustainable?

"Becoming" entails enhancing and improving what we have.

> *"Among the things that distinguish our species from others is our combination of idealism and artistry—our desire both to improve the world and to provide that world with something it didn't know it was missing."[24]*

Daniel H. Pink

Once we are aware of our current practice, the shift to bring about improvement and innovation requires behavioural change. There are three factors that good human system behavioural change should comprise of:

1. A <u>traditional economic incentive</u>. Taxes, waivers and other inducements from government, as well as the simple incentive of an enhanced bottom line.

2. A <u>social incentive</u>. We don't want to be seen by others as doing something wrong. Plus, this is bad for

---

24      Daniel H. Pink, *To Sell is Human: The Surprising Truth About Persuading, Convincing, and Influencing Others* (Edinburgh: Canongate, 2014)

business as more and more customers and shareholders are becoming conscious buyers.

3. A <u>moral incentive</u>. Highly intertwined with the above. We don't want to do something we consider wrong. This one is intrinsic, as you know where you stand, and how it feels to impact your immediate environment—including team, generation and habitat.

**Let's create better value, shall we?**

The aim is to create a world where everyone can live well within its natural limits, that being highly beneficial for your organisation and yes also for the planet. You must put it at the heart of everything you do, including brands, products and behaviours within and beyond your walls (even virtual ones), partnerships and advocacy efforts which are driving transformational change across your value chain.

With the previous section "Anchor" in mind, we need to first know where we are at right now. Then, make shifts as part of our day-to-day routine into what we do. That way, you can become more sustainable, fast. You don't need more long-winded programmes, separate teams, funding or separate budgets focused on meeting traditional economic incentives and guidelines. That will only slow you down.

You can integrate sustainability into every aspect of your supply chain. First, acknowledge how much sustainable practices account for your total emissions. For example, in FY21 66% of Salesforce's GHG emissions came from their suppliers.[25] So, as of April 2021, Salesforce added a Sustainability Exhibit to all supplier procurement contracts with a goal of reducing the

---

25      World's #1 CRM, Salesforce, www.salesforce.com/campaign/worlds-number-one-CRM/

company's collective carbon footprint.[26] This represents the mantra of continuous improvement and, as Salesforce founder and CEO Marc Benioff puts it, "The business of business is improving the state of the world." For those who do not know them, Salesforce is ranked #1 in the world for Customer Relationship Management applications, and achieved over USD 21 billion in annual revenue in their fiscal year of 2021.

Second, embedding new habits into existing ones helps to gradually shift inertia, as resistance will naturally occur in the face of a change to the current state of motion. For any organisation, establishing a long-term commitment in strategy can create initiative and drive; this can transform into momentum like a snowball effect, even when a seemingly small change begins to build upon itself.

It means acquiring new habits in purchasing, in design, in system thinking, patterns, manufacturing, behaviour… you name it. Becoming better at what we do is what Daniel H. Pink refers to *mastery*, the desire to improve.[27] This entails practice, like that required when playing an instrument, with constant feedback loops. It comes from within, so putting it in the hands of only one department or outsourcing it ain't gonna work. For a habit to stick, the 'trick' is to attach it to your current motions, such as locating recycling bins closer to points of use. A plastic recycling bin in the kitchen or paper recycling near a printer could act as a constant reminder near to relevant daily tasks.

Another example of attaching a habit into current motions so that it 'sticks' is one from a framework often used in the

---

26      John Perkins and Ryan Hart, Integrating Sustainability Supply Chain Contracts, Salesforce, www.salesforce.com/content/dam/web/en_us/www/documents/white-papers/integrating-sustainability-supply-chain-contracts.pdf

27      Daniel H. Pink, *Drive: The Surprising Truth About What Motivates Us* (Edinburgh: Canongate, 2018)

technology space, Scrum. At the end of each cycle (let's say a week) there is a Review of the product (like a demo open forum of the product enhancement achieved that week). Straight after there is a Retrospective, both for and by the team, that involves a pause to reflect on the What (the product) and the How (the process). This pause of reflection takes a bit of practice but it soon becomes a habit to pause and reflect on how to improve at how we do things.

Those means of acquiring new habits should be by design, by being attached at the current motions could be including it as part of your life-cycle assessment through the whole value chain, in the agreements for new partnerships, or in supplier contracts, enabling all stakeholders to achieve and maintain the levels of operation and certification required to support your shared sustainability goals.

You can apply a healthy pressure to partners and suppliers to rethink their environmental behaviour. This can cover anything from packaging and recycling to reducing travel times and distances, whether by air, rail or road. What are their mitigation efforts? This will have an impact on your footprint across the value chain. It's in your best interest to apply pressure and provide help there.

Extend this healthy pressure to other areas, such as hours worked. Being sustainable is not just about the product itself and how we deliver it—it's also about the people involved. I often see third party consultants being expected to work mad hours; not just by the project, but by their employers too. This has to be nipped in the bud, and it can easily be done by you. It's not acceptable behaviour, so do not tolerate it. In fact, it is in the declaration of Human Rights. Article 24 states that: "Everyone has the right to rest and leisure, including reasonable limitation of working hours and periodic holidays with pay."[28] Being overworked or underworked is just nonsense. Yet we see it and experience it way too often. It's not good for your health, focus, concentration, happiness or effectiveness, and it can't be maintained over time. In other words, it's unsustainable.

Working long hours, long weeks and long months doesn't *get more done.* And certainly, whatever is being done is unlikely to be better. On the contrary, it tends to be much lower in quality. It's a draining pace that has a detrimental effect on mood, stamina and intelligence. In fact, it can impact your whole life. Life is perishable; we should treat every moment with the care that it deserves. Being ephemeral, it isn't coming back. So, look after yourself, go home and switch off, and help your team and the rest of your organisation to do the same.

> *"Creating the culture of burnout is opposite to creating a culture of sustainable creativity."[29]*
>
> Arianna Huffington

I'm just planting the seed here; we'll come back to this in Part Two.

---

28    Universal Declaration of Human Rights, United Nations, www.un.org/en/about-us/universal-declaration-of-human-rights#:~:text=Article%2024,and%20periodic%20holidays%20with%20pay.

29    Arianna Huffington, as quoted by Ekaterina Walter in *8 Life And Leadership Lessons From Arianna Huffington,* Forbes, https://www.forbes.com/sites/ekaterinawalter/2013/09/03/8-life-and-leadership-lessons-from-arianna-huffington/?sh=5df47ce160c7

## How can we make that leap from physical into digital?

Another area of focus that can make a big difference to our sustainability (yes, including profit), in energy use is the move into offering digital products and services.

According to the IEA, the energy use by leading tech firms is relatively minor compared with their economic, financial and social footprint.[30] Indeed, data centres account for around 1% of global electricity use, which is significantly lower than the roles that industrial motors or air conditioning businesses have as drivers on global electricity demand.

Moving to digital has a direct effect on greenhouse emissions, as digital products and services do not have to be wrapped or sent around the world. The capital lifetime of those is different. With physical items your aim is for them to last longer, be retired less often and replaced less over time; digital products, in contrast, are essentially ephemeral ideas, whose very architecture by abstraction and decoupling can make them almost infinitely flexible to be reused, recreated or discarded. Build to adapt, not to last.

Since moving away from physical products also reduces the extraction of new materials, let's think about recreating instead of 'lift and shift'. Have a good look at your material sourcing; at the waste on its production, on your return process and how items come back into the value chain. How can it be leaner, whilst reducing your carbon footprint?

In terms of digitising your offering, we can look at Banco do Brasil as an example; founded over 200 years ago, today it is the largest financial institution in Latin America. Banco do Brasil does not limit itself to the traditional role of a lending agent, rather it sees itself as a catalyst for sustainable development in the country. The bank offers a range of environmentally and

---

30      *Global Data Centre Energy Demand By Data Centre Type, 2010-2022,* IEA, www.iea.org/data-and-statistics/charts/global-data-centre-energy-demand-by-data-centre-type-2010-2022

socially responsible products and services for its clients, such as special investment funds, and lines of credit for investments in sustainable agricultural activities, forestation and reforestation, agro-ecology, organic production and the reduction and absorption of GHGs.

They have undertaken a holistic approach to their operations and go-to-market strategy, which you can see by looking at just one of their efforts; for their paper efficiency program, they have achieved 22.3% paper consumption reduction compared to 2018, which corresponds to 1.2 tons less paper, preventing approximately 12,700 trees from being cut down.[31]

Through a digital transformation of processes and awareness-raising which engage and guide your employees, you could reduce your consumption of A4 paper and paper receipt reels. This gives you opportunities to use less paper in your day-to-day office activities, even if that office is at home. You can develop a campaign in your company, such as "think before printing". Then, show your colleagues and customers how they contribute to climate change by providing an average measure of paper consumption per employee and client annually. After all, from the very moment you print something, since the physical document is static the information becomes obsolete and stale.

The fact is that the leap from physical into digital offerings is already happening. Look at your own communication efforts; we have shifted from having your target audiences consuming outbound content to the content itself being interactive instead, so that they can participate. Marketing is now about delivering services, rather than passive information. Everything from blogs and whitepapers to calculators and quizzes are all examples of this. As are services that help customers to measure their own consumption of products, those are also digital

---

31      GEE Inventory, Banco Brasil, www45.bb.com.br/rao/ri/ra2017/en/inventario-gee.html

offerings. It's also about a mindset shift from ownership to access.

Whether we like it or not, software is a vehicle for scale and sustainability. Technology can really help to deliver better value along a continuum which consequently optimises your products and services. With it, you can go to market earlier, get feedback earlier, and base your next efforts on that actual information from market reaction rather than assumptions; that enables you to deliver what is really wanted.

So, it is dynamic. A mindset that helps to depict the reality of the continuum we live in requires us to think about products and procedures rather than projects; whilst a product is in the market and in use, it can only get better at adapting to the changes in its environment.

At the time of writing this, I had the pleasure of attending and speaking at London's Calling.[32] They always have very interesting and thought-provoking keynotes. This year's keynote was Ben Hammersley, the founder and principal of Hammersley Futures, who specialises in analysing how society reacts to technological innovation.[33] He considers areas such as the future of crime and conflict, the changing nature of the workplace and market and the new cognitive tools needed to flourish in the coming decades. Hammersley is a futurist. In his keynote he made a powerful analogy. He highlighted the Andon Cord; a device implemented on Toyota assembly lines which, when pulled, stopped all production immediately. The principle behind the Andon Cord was that if a problem was identified then a complete stop of production until it

---

32      London's Calling is the largest community-led yearly conference for Salesforce professionals with over 400 in-person attendees and 8000 virtual attendees. www.londonscalling.net

33      *Announcing the London's Calling Keynote Speaker for 2021,* London's Calling, www.londonscalling.net/announc-ing-the-londons-calling-keynote-speaker-for-2021-ben-hammer-sley

was properly solved encouraged more output in the long run than trying to continue working and problem-solving simultaneously. Hammersley views COVID-19 as an Andon Cord for our workplace systems. A pause. A shift of 10 years of progress in 10 days. And a reassessment of everything. This links to the previous section, Anchor, where businesses have had to re-evaluate how they do things.

By reflecting on the past 18 months of the COVID-19 pandemic, and the rollercoaster that has affected our world and understanding the fundamental shifts and implications of those, we can start to understand and build on what's going to happen in the future, allowing our companies to become something new. Technology and the digital world are there to solve problems—it can make it or break it, it's up to us.

More than ever, we can make a difference in the technology space. In fact, these recent shifts have demonstrated how, through their technological choices, many companies have been living in a different time from others; as Hammersley prompted us to assess, "Try to think about precisely what year your organisation lives in," as when looking at behavioural practices there are many still living in the past.

Fight the urge to just react: be curious, ask questions and challenge the status quo. Cultivating curiosity helps us to think more deeply and widely about things, this is what prompts us to come up with more creative options. It's essential to remember that we can't apply a deterministic mindset to an emergent area. For now, all we can do is trial, test and tweak accordingly.

For this to work, we need to operate with small and rapid feedback loops built into the fabric of what we do, make decisions quickly based on evidence and have the ability to adjust course and respond quickly. After all, nowadays competitive advantage is based on two things: fast time to market, and experimentation as an operational fabric (so that you can test business ideas quickly, and decide whether to pivot or persevere). We'll come back to this in Part Three.

# C is for Collaborate

Teams can work fast, really fast. But if the rest of the organisation does not keep up the pace, it defeats the object.

What else do you do today that can be digitalised? Digital solutions can be a great enabler; we've already seen that the shift into digital products and services can make a big difference to our sustainability. It's key that we keep going in this arena within our organisations, we must be smarter when doing so.

As you digitise your offerings, you also digitise internally. One of the most common myths is to believe that IT is just an output department; it is instead at the core of your goal. Your goal as an organisation is to maximise flow—the movement of potential value through your system.

From a McKinsey study in 2018, we learn that the most commonly cited objective for digital transformations is digitising the organisation's operating model (68% of respondents), while less than half said that their objective was either to launch new products or services, or to interact with external partners through digital channels.[34]

In the second quarter of 2019, Banco do Brasil reached 3.3 million clients with its digital bank, a rise of 11.9% from the same period of 2018. In addition, during the first half of 2019,

---

34    *Unlocking Success in Digital Transformations,* McKinsey & Company, www.mckinsey.com/business-functions/organiza-tion/our-insights/unlocking-success-in-digital-transformations#

79% of all transactions by Banco do Brasil clients were made via digital channels.[35]

If we look at Ørsted, they also rely on a digital strategy that includes advanced analytics and artificial intelligence (AI) technology. It helps the company transform data from its 1,300 offshore wind turbines into insights for predictive maintenance that in turn save time and resources. This digitalisation is a huge challenge in offshore wind, and yet it is key to keeping operational costs at an efficient level.

Digital transformations tend to be wide in scope. And *transformation* is such a heavy word, which comes with a lot of baggage—I much prefer digital evolution (not revolution). In the McKinsey study mentioned earlier, eight out of ten respondents mentioned that their recent change efforts involved multiple functions, business units, or the whole enterprise. If you want to go far, go together.

There's no single piece of technology or software that enables digital evolution. It is a combination of cultural, as well as technological change which leads to the improved performance, effectiveness and flow of your system.

The flow of your entire system, yes! Organisations are operating systems. You will quickly realise (if you haven't yet) that a very small number of resources are dictating the pace of flow of the entire system. This means that you are not delivering to the full capacity that is already available to you, therefore there is waste in your system.

And waste, whichever interpretation of the word you think of, hinders any efforts towards being sustainable.

The holistic flow of your operating system should be regenerative by design. As outlined in the concept we lightly touched on earlier, a circular economy facilitates continuous

---

35      *Banco do Brasil turning into a digital player,* bnamericas, www.bnamericas.com/en/features/banco-do-brasil-is-turning-into-a-digital-player

inspection and adaptation, in order to reduce waste and maximise what you have.[36]

If we think of the legacy production model—deterministic input and output—we think of a linear process which is not sustainable because:

- We have limited raw materials which will eventually run out.

- Waste accumulates, which incurs expenses related to disposal and causes pollution.

- Manufacturing processes are often themselves inefficient, leading to further waste of natural resources.

- Returns processes are often themselves inefficient, leading to further pollution and materials decay.

There is a relevant link between profits, recycling and the potential savings. For example, in sectors such as manufacturing complex, medium-lived products (like mobile phones), the annual net-materials cost savings are estimated to be up to USD 630 billion.[37]

In a circular economy, materials for new products come from old products. As much as possible, everything is reused, remanufactured or, as a last resort, recycled back into a raw material or used as a source of energy. In our organisation's operating systems we should aim to capture the flow of materials, nutrients, components and products, whilst adding an element of financial value.

---

36      *Circular Economy,* Wikipedia, www.en.wikipedia.org/wiki/Circular_economy

37      *Towards the Circular Economy,* Ellen MacArthur Foundation,      www.ellenmacarthurfoundation.org/assets/downloads/publications/Ellen-MacArthur-Foundation-Towards-the-Circular-Economy-vol.1.pdf

When we talk about circular thinking and eco-design, plastics are a substantial issue of the "final stage" of production cycles. Ocean plastic pollution is a big concern worldwide. This is another area where we can make conscious day-to-day decisions which can make the much-needed difference. Later, we'll learn how Ecoalf is leading approaches to tackle this matter. For now, I point you to this comprehensive entry from the UK Government site: www.gov.uk/managing-your-waste-an-overview.

Remember how, around March 2020, your organisation made it possible to adapt in a fraction of the time that a change of that magnitude would have required in other circumstances? How many processes have been digitised, have moved forward and accelerated at a rate you've never seen before?

**Where and how to look?**

As humans, we have the tendency to look for answers where it is the easiest and most comfortable for us to do so.

This occurs when the searcher's ability is compromised when tackling the subject, collecting or analysing data, and their mind is geared towards their *safe space*. It's a type of observational bias. This inertia has been named The Streetlight Effect and it goes something like this:

"What are you doing?"

"Searching for my keys."

"Did you lose them here?"

"No, I lost them over there, but the light is much better here."[38]

You can see this phenomenon in organisations all around, where the overarching vision is split into departmental goals. Everyone splinters into groups and, with the best of intentions, does their own thing.

---

38      *Streetlight effect,* Wikipedia, https://en.wikipedia.org/wiki/Streetlight_effect

This behaviour has a relatively simple antidote. Simple to understand, difficult to master. The first step is being aware of this tendency at an individual level. The second is to have a good dose of curiosity.

Curiosity may have killed the cat, but it can revive your organisation. Arguing over positions produces unwise outcomes, which can range anywhere from complete polarisation to begrudging compromise. Both are incredibly inefficient, as they need much back and forth from the parties involved and worse it endangers ongoing relationships. I've been there: it's ugly, unhelpful and unhealthy.

We get stuck on our own ideas and when the reality doesn't match that we don't always take it very well. Getting detached from being attached to one's own ideas is tough. We need a different angle to see through a lens of curiosity. Rather than trying to suppress an inner voice, use this new perspective to open up and reach a new understanding.

I have come to realise that asking is so much more powerful than talking. Cultivating curiosity helps us to think more deeply and widely about things, and that enables us to come up with more creative options.

Being curious in meetings, in interviews, approaching a promotion, a bid, a challenge; this fosters innovation. It's about helping our minds to open up, seek understanding and, in a sense, be playful.

As an added bonus, it's also good for your health. A 2005 report in the journal Health Psychology found that higher levels of curiosity were also associated with a decreased chance of developing conditions such as diabetes and hypertension.[39]

Curiosity is an important part of evolving your digital products, services and operations. To understand deeply how things

---

39      L. S. Richman, L. Kubzansky, J. Maselko, I. Kawachi, P. Choo, and M. Bauer, *Positive Emotion and Health: Going Beyond the Negative,* Health Psychology, 24, (2005), page 422-429

work and craft a better way, it is essential to compartmentalise, structure, frame and scale; allowing computing to process it. What is this for? Why do we do it like this? Why do we do it at all? Crafting the flow of your organisation with deep understanding.

How can you then apply this curiosity to depict collaboratively your entire business flow?

### Draw a picture together

Yes literally, what is your current circular economy? What does it look like? Draw it with your teams so that it depicts the current state, so that you can better craft your vision. It becomes a representation that gives clarity, alignment and collaboration as a whole of where you are going.

When I often do this exercise with organisations, at first we get disparity yet, with some perseverance we get a picture to refer back to. A picture which has crafted a common understanding and a set of principles to guide our acts towards the vision. A system map.

It works because it helps to step outside of our individual view which has limited information of what can be seen from a single place in the system. Giving perspective and reducing favouring one's own position. Providing better and more complete illustration.

It enables you to define a set of objectives and clearly defined outcomes for your organisation and team to judge itself on performance. In line with that collective team goal, which is to maximize the flow of your entire system.

That is your win, thinking beyond profit, look at your current flow and find the bottlenecks that rule your throughput. With perspective, allow yourself to see the forest through the trees.

What does your system map look like today? If you were an outsider only looking at its behaviour, what would you deduce its purpose to be? Current actual behaviour rather than the desired one. What would you guess the structure was set up to do?

To maximise your flow, you need to decide what is important, what matters and what doesn't. Look at that picture. What is the bottleneck that dictates your end-to-end system map? Focus on connective structures over individual components. Bring focus, it needs to always be working on your higher priority. A priority which needs to be aligned with the enterprise vision. For that to happen, all the noise needs to be removed.

The thing is, we have the tendency to try to go beyond the capacity of throughput. This leads to diminishing the flow in many ways: operations delivery firefighting; problematic quality of work; very long lead times to get anything done, and so on. After all, things being finished and in use is what brings value, having many things in progress does not.

Even with the best intentions, we are often our own worst enemy. Hence the importance of having integrated landscape approaches, so that they bring clarity and cohesion.

Remember the life-cycle assessment? Embed the information from that effort into your system map, the picture that you have drawn together on how your circular economy looks today.

Systems are non-linear, don't try to force it. What are the balancing loops in your system? Are all feedback loops set up so that they are able to serve the same goal?

Similar to a Kanban system,[40] with these practices working in tandem:

---

40      Kanban is a Japanese word that literally means visual sign. Taiichi Ohno, an industrial engineer at Toyota, developed Kanban as a system to improve efficiency focused on just-in-time manufacturing. *Kanban,* Wikipedia, www.en.wikipedia.org/wiki/Kanban

- Define and visualise a workflow

- Actively monitor items in a workflow

- Improve the workflow

Build your Kanban board

*Figure 1.1: Build your Kanban board examples.*

The examples shown in Figure 1.1 depict two different fairly simplified workflows. One is monitoring items moving through the system from columns New, Make, Deliver to Done as an end state. The second version shows the process from Doing to Options and Done as end column state.

Our brains are wired for visuals.

> *"Seeing comes before words. The child looks and recognizes before it speaks."[41]*

John Berger

Use that system map as an information radiator, to refer back to and to help to make decisions and to reduce deviation from your vision. Refine it and keep it alive as you progress.

---

41      John Berger, *Ways of Seeing* (London: Penguin, 1972)

If you are to improve it, redesign the system so that it improves the flow of information, the goals and most importantly the value it generates. Look to reduce constraints and stresses as well as observe the incentives and disincentives that surface. A redesign so that your system serves a common more important goal that every bit can support as one towards the same purpose. Keeping in mind that system flows do take time to change.

### Don't do it alone

In March 2010 Banco do Brasil defined the conservation of water resources as the principal focus of its sustainability initiatives. Agua Brasil ("The Brazil Water Programme") is an example of how Banco do Brasil is exploring connections among water conservation, good agricultural practices, environmental restoration, forest conservation and climate change adaptation and mitigation.

This nexus is an important one in the Brazilian context, given that 29% of land in the country is dedicated to agricultural-livestock production activities, 82% of Brazil's water is consumed by the rural sector, and Brazil is anticipating adverse impacts of climate change to affect both water resources and the agricultural sector.

In 2010, Banco do Brasil forged a partnership with the National Water Agency (ANA) and the World Wide Fund for Nature–Brasil to develop the Agua Brasil programme. For the pilot projects, the partners have identified 14 important watersheds, located in the Cerrado/Pantanal, Atlantic Forest, Amazonia, Caatinga and Pampa biomes. Pilot projects involve the creation of local water management plans, including water footprinting and training of basin committees and other stakeholders on improved watershed management.

Agua Brasil enables Banco do Brasil to benefit from the new business opportunities that result from its expanded range of climate-resilient products and services, as it uses its power within the banking industry to influence the practices of current and new clients. Farmers will have access to an expanded range of financial products and services (including credit), that both incentivise and assist them with implementing these sustainable farming techniques, thereby improving their livelihoods.

Banco do Brasil, the World Wild Fund-Brazil and the National Water Agency have been working together on this programme since 2011, involving 150 partners across all regions of the country. They have focused on minimising the impacts of economic activities by improving new credit granting criteria for business development, which are able to contribute to society and the environment. Caring for the soil in a sustainable way is done by means of training programmes for producers, which provide social technologies that can be applied in pilot projects. It would not have been possible to do that without the collaboration of more than 150 thousand organisations involved around the country.

The stories behind the effort from the farmers and ranchers involved in this project look at the results of their own actions over time to achieve sustainable practices, and as a result they earn credits to support sustainable production. This shows that public and private agencies can be part of social changes in a big country like Brazil. The project also takes into account the fact that economic and social awareness can create large sustainable business opportunities, which are happening right now.[42] These efforts can stimulate a low carbon economy, by generating incomes for social inclusion, sustainable economic growth and nature conservation.

Collaboration towards a common goal enriches the experience and outcomes, while also increasing its potential and influence.

---

42        Programa Água Brasil, *Programa Água Brasil,* YouTube, www.youtube.com/watch?v=ixoCtPCT7Qs

> *As a side note on enriching, at a nutrition level, you may want to enrich your diet too by increasing the proportion of it which comes from plant-based. From a carbon emissions perspective, it is significantly better for the environment to do so, with wider implications on the reduction of water use. In addition to the commonly known benefits to one's own health.*

Lean manufacturing has much to teach us about collaboration. One element of this is working together very closely with suppliers, for example, with the main purpose of waste reduction. Here, openness and collaboration goes beyond what we may be used to. Having information symmetry may mean gathering some of your most knowledgeable subject-specific people and going to help one of your third parties with an all-hands-on-deck approach.

Swarming. A common concept from lean practices, which I define as: "The act of a group jumping in to solve a problem, get things done, through self organisation and decentralisation. It reminds me of one of the many things we can learn from lean manufacturing, the benefits of leaving roles and hierarchies aside and jumping in as a group with a common goal to work something out."[43] We don't see or do this enough, we must break through.

The whole is in fact greater than the sum of its parts.

**Influence your Systems Architecture**

Systems thinking is a concept we hear often. It's relevant enough—every conversation that we have is, at least in part, governed by the overarching system that encompasses its operations.

Think of an organisation much as you would a natural organism—an organisation is a collective response to its

---

43      Ines Garcia, *Becoming more Agile whilst delivering Salesforce,* (Get Agile Ltd, 2020)

environment and, to survive, it must adapt as the environment changes. In short, it helps us to evolve, grow and thrive.

Systems thinking helps us to understand the relationship between the structure and the behaviour. Systems architecture encompasses the structure of the operating system, the way in which it interrelates, the shape given, the arrangement of internal components, and the way in which those components communicate. All of these elements help to form the way that the system is organised, its networks, and the behaviours that take place within it.

This all boils down to the fact that our workplace systems are forged on relationships. Connective power. These relationships have the ability to impact and influence one another, so this capacity can be leveraged to bring about change in a more organic, long-lasting way. Evolution, not revolution.

Mapping this architecture out as an image, as we covered, is a great way to shed new light on the connections, and better understand how your own systems operate. Draw it abstractly enough so that it's easy to digest, and complete enough so that it's useful—information balance.

As the tendency of human nature dictates, we have obsessed for decades on its components, on the details. As a result, all too often, we focus on minute details, and miss the whole picture. Try creating these area maps of your systems side by side, then think about how different systems communicate with each other.

What do they have in common? You can understand this as a cultural system—an organisation is a mini-society, with its own culture and subcultures defined by their values, norms, beliefs, and rituals. In fact, the purpose of this shape influences far more factors than you may initially realise. It affects the development of your product and services, its deployment (how easy it is to get it in the hands of your users), and your entire system map, including the maintenance and operation of each single component.

Avoid dependency cycles—series of events regularly repeated and hooked with each other—on your system architecture, invest time to break dependencies rather than manage them. We need to hold a deep awareness that the forces that shape the system architecture are technical, political and unstable.

We are trying to put modules around things to help us, when we are working with the most non-modular character and deal with the least linear thing of all, humans.

An effective system map is one that delivers what customers want, when they want it. It allocates available economic resources as optimally as possible to deliver value and increases predictability of workflow whilst controlling risk, which allows you to forecast delivery of value within an acceptable degree of uncertainty, reinforcing good behaviours and impact.

The primary purpose of your system architecture is a network-oriented view to support its own lifecycle. Let's take the human brain. On the one hand, it is a complex organisation made up of a number of systems, processes, nerves, thoughts, and emotions. Take a step back to look at its entirety and you see a set of functions designed to process information and learn over time.

With this in mind, a good system is one which is:

- Easy to understand
- Easy to develop
- Easy to deploy
- Easy to maintain
- Easy to enhance
- Easy to adapt

The system should self-elevate its own behaviour and lift its network-capability to a level that simplifies the understanding of it, which significantly helps its own adaptability and maintenance.

# Call. Be. Act.

*"Climate change is the biggest, most important and most complex challenge humans have ever faced, and we know right now, every individual, every company needs to step forward and do everything it can."[44]*

Patrick Flynn

We've now got to the end of our Sustainable ABCs; Anchor, Become and Collaborate. Let's recap on the things that you can start today:

**Find out where you are currently at**

Measure your business's:

- Electricity emissions

- Business travel type: air, ground, hotel, rental cars, etc.

- Fleet vehicle changes and rotation

- Carbon emissions, start with WWF Footprint Calculator or *carbonfootprint.com/measure.html.* The

---

44      Patrick Flynn is the VP of sustainability at Salesforce. He is quoted here by Ron Miller, in *Salesforce is building an app to gauge a company's sustainability progress,* TechCrunch, www.techcrunch.com/2019/09/18/salesforce-is-developing-an-app-to-help-build-a-sustainable-company

company who developed it have reduced their own emissions per unit turnover by 89% from their initial baseline.

## Compare your consumption

The International Performance Measurement and Verification Protocol (IPMVP) is an international methodology that certified professionals recommend be applied to businesses for consumption comparison: www.evo-world.org/en/products-services-mainmenu-en/protocols/ipmvp. Here are some examples of companies offering that service:

- www.ukenergywatch.co.uk
- www.currant.com
- www.sparkcognition.com
- www.solvewithvia.com
- www.ambyint.com
- www.raptormaps.com
- www.sapient.industries/solutions
- www.waypoint-energy.com

## Make key changes

Switch to renewable energies and hydroelectricity; reduce travel (both air and motor mileage); reduce electricity use, either with smart plugs or by switching appliances off when not in use. From the measured findings where else could you make a switch?

Favour repair over replace. Find out more about this through, for example, the NGO Waste and Resources Action Programme.[45] You can also read about blockchain projects within the waste

---

45      *Taking Action: The way we live today is damaging our planet,* Wrap, www.wrap.org.uk/taking-action

management sector at www.swachhcoin.com. A simple way to make a key change is to aim to achieve a constant of zero-food waste in the workplace.

**Start a life-cycle assessment of your value chain**

You can start by identifying your processes and checking whether your raw materials could be certified as sustainable sources, like Ørsted did. I would highly recommend going through the Global Guidance Principle as it covers everything from inventory analysis to impact assessment and categories, interpretation, data flow maps, dataset process, aggregation, and more![46] You can use tools such as the Simple LCA,[47] or the Ghg Protocol,[48] which is applicable to many businesses, regardless of their sector.

**Seek a sustainable certification**

This will help you to understand the specification and how to attain it, so that you can verify that you are meeting high standards of social and environmental performance, public transparency and legal accountability, in order to balance profit with purpose. For example a certification such as B-Corps who also have a handy assessment tool for you to use.[49]

---

46      *Global Guidance Principles for Life Cycle Assessment Databases: A Basis for Greener Processes and Products*, Life Cycle Initiative, www.lifecycleinitiative.org/wp-content/uploads/2012/12/2011%20-%20Global%20Guidance%20Principles.pdf

47      *Simple LCA*, EC Europa, ec.europa.eu/environment/archives/emas/toolkit/downloads/5_1_lca.pdf

48      *Calculation Tools*, GHG Protocol, www.ghgprotocol.org/calculation-tools#cross_sector_tools_id

49      *About B Corps*, B Corporation, www.bcorporation.net/about-b-corps

These certifications are helping to accelerate a global culture shift, which redefines success in business, and builds a more inclusive and sustainable economy. It reinforces the fact that the future is up to us.

You can also assess the MultiCapital Scorecard,[50] a free and open-source management tool that organisations can use to measure, manage and report their performance in a fully integrated way (Triple Bottom Line).

| Bottom Lines | Areas of Impact | Capital Impacts | A B C D D-C | C/D | TBL Scores |
|---|---|---|---|---|---|
| | Worker Safety | ● ◉ ● | 3 3 9 9 0 | 100% | |
| Social | Product Safety | ● | -1 3 -3 9 12 | -33% | 50% |
| | TBL Reporting | ◉ ● | 3 2 6 6 0 | 100% | |
| | Living Wage | ◉ | 2 2 4 6 2 | 67% | |
| Economic | Shareholder Returns | ● | 3 1 3 3 0 | 100% | 87% |
| | Debt | ◉ | 3 2 6 6 0 | 100% | |
| | Climate | ● | 1 3 3 9 6 | 33% | |
| Environmental | Solid Waste | ● | 2 1 2 3 1 | 67% | 53% |
| | Water Use | ● | 3 1 3 3 0 | 100% | |
| A-D Professional Performance & Weighting Scores Triple Bottom Line (TBL) | Grand Totals & TBL Score | | 18 33 54 | | 61% |

Vital capitals:
Economic  Notfinancial    Internal Extenal    ● Natural    ◉ Constructed
 ■■◖○                         ●◖▭              ● Human      ◉ Social & Relationship

*Figure 1.2: Sample implementation of the MultiCapital Scorecard™. Adapted from www.multicapitalscorecard.com*

The scorecard shown in Figure 1.2 is used to analyse vital social, economic and environmental capitals. The social stand includes worker and product safety, and Triple Bottom Line (TBL) reporting. The economic strand considers the living wage, shareholder returns and debt. The environmental strand measures impact on climate, solid waste and water usage. The scorecard allows the company to judge the impact of their production or service on the natural world, constructed objects,

---

50      *MultiCapital Scorecard,* MultiCapital Scorecard, www. multicapitalscorecard.com/multicapital-scorecard/

systems or ecosystems, human or social and relationship within and beyond the company, as well as whether these impacts are internal or external, economic or non-financial. For each section, the company must work out a score for their context which then allows them to calculate a total TBL score.

**Compensate**

The aim is to cut carbon emissions 'at source' as much as possible, so in your journey to become sustainable, you can compensate for emissions you have not yet managed to control with carbon offsetting. This is not the go-to solution, because it doesn't deal with the problem at heart, it's only a temporary *top up* to render your activities carbon neutral.

Some tools to measure your carbon footprint can be found at:

- www3.epa.gov/carbon-footprint-calculator
- www.carbontrust.com/resources/sme-carbon-footprint-calculator
- www.coolclimate.org/business-calculator

> *"As we look ahead, the central objective of the United Nations for 2021 is to build a truly Global Coalition for Carbon Neutrality."[51]*

UN Secretary-General António Guterres

Your first rapid shift should be to source your energy supply away from fossil fuels and into renewables. Then, you can start lean practices towards resource-efficient circular material across your system map, becoming leaner and remaking with less

---

51      *Summit shows new surge in action and ambition on road to Glasgow Climate Conference,* Gov.uk, www.gov.uk/government/news/summit-shows-new-surge-in-action-and-ambition-on-road-to-glasgow-climate-conference?utm_source=3f89a0ef-cac8-423b-8712-69771554195d

stuff, and repairing items from your returns process. It's then that you can make the organisational switch to the creation of ideas as products and services, rather than physical things. Even as a manufacturer, how can you reduce waste? How to minimise use of new materials? How to produce on demand? How to diversify digital offerings over further physical ones?

**Get perspective**

Use things like value stream mapping and zoom in/out exercises to scale the concept of epics to suit your value streams.[52] Use Kanban boards as a visual representation of your flow. Start by understanding your main bottleneck, and what your actual throughput rhythm looks like. Acquire the mantra of valuing finishing over starting, and maximise your flow.

Think about kicking off a Green Team, creating an employee group within your organisation to champion this, not as a silo, but as a driving force for good. They can help with identifying areas and opportunities within your operating system, whilst bringing awareness and engagement, so that it becomes a part of the fabric of your organisation.

> *"When we look at what is truly sustainable, the only real model that has worked over long periods of time is the natural world."*[53]

> Janine Benyus

---

52      *Epic*, Agile Alliance, www.agilealliance.org/glossary/epic

53      *What isn't biomimicry?*, Biomimicry Institute, www.bio-mimicry.org/what-is-biomimicry

# Part Two

# Happy

*"Happy people simply do better - at home, at work, in life."*[54]

Jeff Sutherland

On the other side of the coin, someone once said that stress makes people stupid. It's certainly a thing, surely you can recall situations which support this? At work, at home, and anywhere in between: let's not neglect the emotional aspect when managing the cognitive one.

To me this neglect becomes especially apparent in a workplace phenomenon that's often called *reorganisation*, an overhaul of a company's internal structure. Reorg after reorg, things don't appear to get better, in fact they get worse. My theory is that more often than not, we are guilty of being oblivious of feelings. And well, in this particular scenario of reorgs, there is also a lack of systems thinking. Why do we do it like this?

To acknowledge the reasons and effects that can arise from a lack of happiness, first we need to make sure that we can successfully gauge where we are with it. What's the state of affairs? Are people paid well? Is treatment fair? This is the sort of information that you won't be able to see on your traditional financial reports.

---

54      Jeff Sutherland, *Scrum: The art of doing twice the work in half the time* (London: Random House Business, 2015)

At a macro level there are other ways to measure our social and economic development. "Happiness Economics" and "Gross National Happiness" are both part of the same disruptive framework, which facilitates more accurate discussions about welfare, while avoiding being too narrow minded. As with the correlation we discussed on GDP, this figure is not the only element that we can consider when assessing whether or not we have a healthy economy. On the contrary, there is much to account for.

For example, the Happy Planet Index uses a simple method to calculate and show its results, which only considers four dimensions and their associated ratios.[55] On the other hand, the World Happiness Report seems to be more complex in terms of methodology, because it uses a multivariate regression (econometrics), which is not so friendly for an average muggle like me, yet it is still important to consider it as another way to tackle the same measurement.[56]

Talking about metrics, we need to bear in mind Campbell's Law when assessing the impact of social change.[57] According to this law, "the more quantitative social indicator is used for social decision-making, the more subject it will be to corruption pressures and the more apt it will distort and corrupt the social processes it is intended to monitor." Remember the three flavours of incentives? Economic, social and moral. For these metrics, use a combination of both quantitative and qualitative indicators, as using only quantitative will tend to distort and manipulate the results. Seek value, measure impact.

---

55      *Happy Planet Index,* Happy Planet Index, www.happy-planetindex.org

56      The World Happiness Report is a publication of the Sustainable Development Solutions Network. *The World Happiness Report,* The World Happiness Report, www.worldhappiness.report

57      *Campbell's Law,* Wikipedia, ww.en.wikipedia.org/wiki/Campbell%27s_law

Before we get ahead of ourselves, let's define 'happy'. Here, we are talking of evaluative happiness, which is lasting, sustainable and whole (rather than recent joy, which is temporary and sporadic).

Well-being. Within your organisation, what is the level of satisfaction with life overall? Whether we like it or not, work life spills over into personal life. For either or that entails the social, urban and the natural environments we are part of.

Some may be thinking "I don't have time for this". If this is you, I'll give you a piece of advice I often give myself: In whatever you do, if you are too busy for empathy you need to slow down.

Effectiveness vs efficiency, right? As we touched on in Part One, just doing more of the same and working more hours does not lead us to a better place. Efficiency is about doing more of the same and reducing waste, whilst effectiveness is about doing what matters and doing that well. Going faster doesn't lead us to a better destination. We must work smarter, not just harder.

> *"Insanity is doing the same thing over and over and expecting different results."*[58]

> Albert Einstein

So how can we influence ourselves to be happy? Our team? Our employees? Our partners? Our customers? And does happiness translate into profit? Do companies that treat their employees better inadvertently create a positive effect for their financial performance? It may sound obvious, but unhappiness

---

58      As quoted by Frank Wilczek in *Einstein's Parable of Quantum Insanity,* Scientific American, www.scientificamerican. com/article/einstein-s-parable-of-quantum-insanity

has associated costs which, when brought to light, generate resistance and often dismissal.

Back in 2012, Professor Alex Edmans published a paper based on research about firms listed in the "100 Best Companies to Work For in America".[59] It showed that those companies have outperformed others in annual stock market growth by up to 3.8% per year since 1984 (+89% cumulative). The dataset encompassed quite an extensive time period, including recessions such as the crush of the internet bubble and the 2007-08 financial crisis. So, either in good or bad times, there is evidence that happiness at work is not something one should "cut from the budget". Edmans focused his study in one direction by relating satisfaction one year to returns the next. In this way, his findings showed a clear correlation between staff happiness and company profitability, which should not be misconstrued as a correlation between great stock market performance and happy employees.

Evaluative happiness makes us more productive, creative, helpful, better at providing our service, more focused on quality, better team players, more open, more likeable, more empathetic, more resilient, optimistic, motivated, engaged, energetic, faster at learning and better leaders.

At an organisational level, those traits translate into higher productivity, innovation, lower turnover, talent attraction, lower absenteeism, an increase in customer loyalty, higher involvement and commitment from employees… which also translates into higher profit and stock price. These are results, rather than drivers.

---

59      Alex Edmans, *Data,* London Business School, www.alexedmans.com/data

*Figure 2.1: Happiness outcomes influences organizational outcomes.*

Figure 2.1 illustrates that repercussion of outcomes. Happiness outcomes on the left such as creative, helpful, quality, team... leads to organizational outcomes on the right like productivity, innovation, retention etc.

There is nothing fluffy about happiness at work. At the time of writing this, whilst working with a consultancy for a few months, the CEO confessed to me that at first the concept sounded like baloney, but was then confirming that within just a few weeks, even he found himself happier and could visibly see the repercussions that the change was having to the work he does and the impact in the rest of the organisation. He described the impact as *profound*.

# A is for Acknowledge

We can start to think about how companies are contributing to the day-to-day, to take individual actions, habits and behaviors towards attaining a happier life for *their people*. With people I mean employees, customers, suppliers, partners, communities etc.

Organisations that have sustainability programs which focus on social responsibility, circular economy, innovation fuelled by curiosity, learning by doing, strong relationships with communities, and similarly extend these programs to their partners and supercharge their employee diversity policies, are in fact happier. However, in order to move towards this goal, companies need to honestly acknowledge and evaluate their culture before they can start to move towards the culture they want to build.

Forbes Insights combined a research survey in 2020 of 300 leaders with interviews and public data to discover the link between employee experience, customer experience and revenue growth.[60] The research also covered shifts in leadership priorities post-COVID, and steps for aligning employee experience with customer experience. Proving there is a clear relationship between the two, which ultimately impacts your bottom line. The study reports a 1.8 times faster revenue

---

60      Vala Afshar, *The experience equation: Happy employees and customers accelerate growth,* ZDNet, www.zdnet.com/article/the-experience-equation-happy-employees-and-customers-accelerate-growth

growth in organisations where there is high value care and focus on employee experience and customer experience; yet only 76% are to focus on employee experience within the next three years. I'd argue, why not start reaping those benefits sooner? All-in and starting right now.

According to a global study by Towers Watson, the single biggest driver of engagement is whether or not employees feel their managers are genuinely interested in their well-being.[61] While employee engagement reviews focus on increasing employee engagement and productivity, they fail to fully analyse and understand employee experience. These reviews unfortunately still look to some like projects or even if it was a schedule of engagement reviews. A project for a mid-long term period of three years!

The reality is that Employee Experience (EX) is still not embedded into the majority of daily operations. If we correlate EX to User Experience (UX) or Customer Experience (CX) there is much of the holistic picture missing. We know that the goal of UX design is to improve customer satisfaction and loyalty through the utility, ease of use, and benefit provided in the interaction with a product; that's accomplished via a range of things such as the product design, the user interface (UI), the user flow, the leanness of processes, it also includes service design and brand strategy. Despite a plethora of competencies, including Needs, Usability, Information architecture, Interaction design, Visual design, accessibility, desirability in the design and process, it seems that we miss most of the picture when it comes to Employee Experience. Why?

---

61      Steve Nyce and Billie Jean Quade, *Annuities and Retirement Happiness* (Towers Watson, 2012) https://static. fmgsuite.com/media/documents/cb2c32ac-0c76-45d7-bdf2-5566db0b9916.pdf

The research by Towers Watson shows that improving employee happiness raises sales by 37%, productivity by 31% and accuracy of task completion by 19%.

Companies with a culture of employee recognition, where employees feel that their contributions matter, perform better and have less employee turnover than those that don't. For example, Google found that psychological safety, meaning the ability to take risks without fearing the repercussions of failure, was the number one factor shared by the most effective teams in the company.[62] Thriving employees perform 27% better than non-thriving employees, including 89% better on innovation, and they are 79% more committed to the organisation.

It is important that companies develop a clear set of values and outcomes as a frame to work from to ensure they are measuring and monitoring the parts of the business they aim to develop. You get what you measure. For example, having practical techniques that can develop happiness is a skill, transformative in the workplace.

### Culture follows structure

What is the underlying structure of your economic and "political" system? Acknowledge the actual culture, rather than the aspirational one.

Optimising for figures without context leads to trouble. Metrics by themselves mean very little and you just get what you measure. A writer who is paid by the word doesn't have to write quality in order to get paid. A call centre with targets based on call volume does not have to actually give good customer service to 'succeed'. Whilst it is tempting to measure that which is easily measured, is it actually helpful?

---

62      Charles Duhigg, *What Google Learned From Its Quest To Build The Perfect Team,* NY Times, www.nytimes. com/2016/02/28/magazine/what-google-learned-from-its-quest-to-build-the-perfect-team.html?_r=0

> *"Don't go to great trouble to optimize something that never should be done at all. Aim to enhance total systems properties, such as creativity, stability, diversity, resilience, and sustainability—whether they are easily measured or not."*[63]

Kenneth Boulding

As part of an organisation, we make tiny decisions every second; often through the lens of *what is in it for me*. This method of calculation leads many to decisions and behaviours that ultimately have a detrimental effect on the whole. It produces fragmentation rather than the increased integration sought through the process of maximising metrics in silos.

To become more aware of this behavioural tendency, we need to observe and acknowledge how sustainable performance is rewarded; find out what are the consistency of practices and how real is the dimension of organisational values against its daily operations?

We often rely on organisational charts to tell the story, to force motions, to guide decisions. Organisational charts were a tool introduced in the 1800s, a tool that hasn't evolved since. In my opinion, these and other corporate structures are outdated archaic legacy tools that most haven't bothered to reassess.

I instead advocate for embracing an organic, evolving system with interrelated responsible teams that are autonomous and self-organised, with a common mission and clear vision.

Think about management to support rather than dictate. Be there to serve, to unblock obstacles, not to tell people what to do and how to do it. Be there to enable an environment where all skills are needed, with multiple development products overlapping, limiting bottlenecks, reducing many hand-offs and waiting times.

---

63      Attributed by Magnus Ramage and Karen Shipp in *Systems Thinkers* (London: Springer, 2009)

Your team and your colleagues solve much harder things every day. Partner with them.

> *"The shortest distance to customers loving your brand is through employees who love their job."*[64]

Tiffani Bova

A study from Woohoo Inc surfaces that 2 out of 3 people said 80-90% of their work days are neutral at best, and bad at their worst![65] In their previous report in 2015, 19% of respondents reported having a bad day at work every day or almost every day. Ouch!

From that same report, they draw the following top 5 factors which influence a good day:

- Meaningful work that made a positive effect for someone else

- Freedom to work their own way

- Doing work that one is proud of

- Having fun with coworkers

- Doing tasks that one enjoys doing

The study crashes the false common wisdom that external motivation in the form of extrinsic rewards and reprisals is the route to employee happiness.

---

64      Tiffani Bova is Global Customer Growth and Innovation Evangelist at Salesforce. *Tiffani Bova,* Twitter, www.twitter.com/Tiffani_Bova/status/1263391580951633924

65      *Our Study of Good Days at Work,* Woohoo Inc, www.woohooinc.com/happiness-at-work/study-good-work-days

**What sets one apart from complications?**

Setbacks are part of the motions, we need balance and we can't just expect to be at *the top of happiness* all the time.[66] Life has ups and downs, and that tempers the soul.

Over the years, I've grown to believe that persistence, enthusiasm and resilience are key. Not all ideas will work out and that's ok, we are to expect the unexpected, right? Especially in our ever-changing environment, the ability to cope with adversity and still have our passion is very important.

Evaluative happiness also energises us. From the previously mentioned Woohoo Inc report, 71.4% said that having a good day at work positively affected their energy levels, 65.8% experienced lasting effects of evaluative happiness after work and 61.9% said evaluative happiness made them more relaxed and less stressed.

Because it works either way, work life and personal life are intertwined. There is a concept often referred to on the subject as "Work-Life Balance", but as it is intertwined, there isn't the same level of separation that scales have. What if work-life and personal-life were *symbiotic*?

> *"Work is an enormous part of most people's lives, both in terms of time spent and value attached. It seems to me that striving to achieve 'balance' is underselling the value I can derive from things in my life that are so important to me. Balance implies you mustn't do too much of one because it will be to the detriment of the other. Integration doesn't work because it makes things blurred around the edges—when I'm playing with my kids I want to be 100% focused on them and not distracted, and when I'm*

---

66      The *top of happiness* is not a thing. Imagine for a second what being on a high happiness level may mean to you, some may describe it as euphoria, some as undisturbed tranquillity and contentment. It varies.

*delivering something for the business I want to give that all my attention too.*

*I think we should expect something more from these two broad categories of activity in our lives of 'home' and 'work'. I think one should positively enable and facilitate the other. The relationship between home and work is fundamental—it is such an integral part of our lives—it needs to be symbiotic: a dependent and mutually beneficial relationship. Each should make the other better."[67]*

Claire Fox

There are some variables that can directly influence the structure, and therefore culture, of our organisations. Studies from Shalok Schwartz in the 1980s surfaced ten clusters of basic personal values, which were recognised across cultures:

- Self-direction
- Stimulation
- Hedonism
- Achievement
- Power
- Security
- Conformity
- Tradition
- Benevolence
- Universalism

Alongside setbacks, which are part of daily life in organisations, positive environments that create a positive and supportive environment do in fact foster change beyond personal

---

67      Claire Fox, *Work/Life Symbiosis: The Model for Happiness and Balance* (London: LID Publishing, 2015)

behaviours. Namely, collaboration across the team improves, which leads to better recovery from these setbacks. Members acting as problem solvers with a common goal.

In a piece of research from Oxford University Saïd Business School, the evidence presented suggested a strong, positive relationship between employee well-being, employee productivity and firm performance. Therefore, raising the well-being of society is a central goal for policy-makers, and it is a goal that is not in opposition to the interests of businesses. They highlighted that "there is an important role for business leaders to play in being a strong positive force for raising the wellbeing of society."[68]

## Where to look?

The problem is that, in a complex process such as business transformation—or evolution, being my preferred term—many things can go wrong. The complexity of the system can't just be pinned to the single factor of 'culture'.

For an effective diagnosis of the conditions and symptoms, we should look at multiple variables:

- History. The whole series of past events, particularly in relation to the human affairs lens.

- Geopolitics. Relations are influenced by geographical factors, so look at your locations and spaces, including digital ones and how the system is designed and performed.

- Culture. Look at the actual rather than the desired: ideas, customs, social behaviour, inclusion and bureaucracy.

---

68      Christian Krekel, George Ward and Jan Emmanuel De Neve, *Employee Wellbeing, Productivity, and Firm Performance,* Saïd Business School, https://papers.ssrn.com/sol3/papers.cfm?abstract_id=3356581

- Economy. That being the structure, budget allocations and what's justified in terms of profitability.

- Observation. Asking questions and monitoring can certainly help with diagnosis. Remember the holistic view of operations and finding your constraints? Do not forget the local circumstances and context which are highly important.

Some time ago, I came across Buurtzorg, an organisation that challenged the status quo to a degree I haven't seen before.[69] Buurtzorg is a Dutch nursing care company delivering community based health care. A company of more than 10,000 employees with no managers, which grew to that size from 4 staff in just 8 years. Founder Jos de Blok explains that they have not had a single management meeting since they kicked off, and that in his former job they "had a lot of meetings that were only about meetings. Now we just have time to solve the problems." Those thousands of employees are organized in around 800 small autonomous teams of up to 12 nurses within a neighbourhood-sized care area.

It's all about focusing on your mission, your core, on what's needed. Reflecting on what you are doing and constantly trying to do it better. For Buurtzorg, that translates to a nurse-led service approach that generates a yearly turnover of EUR 280 million. As their founder put it, let's avoid complexity. "Even with 9,000 people, it can be a very simple organisation. We must build organisations based on meaningful relationships. When nurses feel happy they will stay healthy and they will do good things."

Well-being depends on a cumulative process of multiple variables, from health and access to health care, living and being in a safe environment, education and building skills, contextual experience and accomplishments through setbacks.

---

69      RSA, *Jos de Blok on Organizational Structures,* YouTube, www.youtube.com/watch?v=BeOrNjwHw58

A business without managers may not be the answer for every company, but an honest analysis of the culture and the willingness to replace current complexity with new ways of working is essential for moving forward, to boost what you do.

# B is for Boost

*"People with well-developed emotional skills are also more likely to be content and effective in their lives, mastering the habits of mind that foster their own productivity; people who cannot marshal some control over their emotional life fight inner battles that sabotage their ability for focused work and clear thought."*[70]

Daniel Goleman

The way that we cope and react to complications makes the difference. Daniel Goldman highlights three applications of emotional intelligence:

- Being able to air grievances as helpful critiques

- Creating an atmosphere in which diversity is valued rather than a source of friction

- Networking effectively

Emotional intelligence is an energy booster, through which we can motivate ourselves and persist through setbacks, regulate our moods so that we get a better headspace to think, and be more open, all so that we can empathise and collaborate.

It's an action booster. In a way it makes it more desirable, satisfactory and effective at what we do.

---

70      Daniel Goleman, *Emotional intelligence: Why it can matter more than IQ* (London: Bloomsbury Publishing, 1996)

That all sounds like common sense, right? Yet we mentioned inertia earlier. Inertia can also play a different role, a worrisome one, in our organisations.

When we are presented with complications and unexpected changes, we have the tendency to become more rigid and more bureaucratic. Let me explain, when key backbones and critical items in our organisation are threatened, in ways such as:

- Revenue endangered
- Detrimental disturbance to operations
- Running costs increased
- External brand damage

The immediate reaction is to go into a spiral of self-destruction. We react with fear and, to tame that fear, we impose excessively complicated administrative procedures. In turn that slows us down, with more approvals and checkpoints, more meetings and reports, more tightly coupled and complex coordination. All of this slows our operating system down—meaning we do less, we learn less, we adapt less, therefore ending up worse off.

Here is another symptom to watch out for. We get tangled in routines of the day to day, going through the motions, just as we did yesterday and foresee ourselves doing the next day. This spoils any chances to be better. The so-called status quo. It creeps in. This is a natural tendency, as there is only so much *new* that the human brain can handle, so it goes into autopilot.

One more symptom—this one looking beyond the individual— is the fundamental attribution error,[71] where we tend to read others' actions on a negative incline which we directly relate to their character and their personality. You see this within teams, across teams and departments. At a team level, what I have seen

---

71      Also known as correspondence bias or attribution effect. *Fundamental Attribution Error,* Wikipedia, www./en.wikipedia. org/wiki/Fundamental_attribution_error

working well to break through this tendency is a brief reminder to separate the people from the problem; it goes like this:

> *"Regardless of what we discover, we understand and truly believe that everyone did the best job they could, given what they knew at the time, their skills and abilities, the resources available, and the situation at hand."[72]*

Norman L. Kerth

Although the above is most often used around team retrospectives, it's a powerful concept and it is useful to remind oneself of it. It sets the scene of participants as problem solvers with a common goal. It detaches egos, as so easily we get stuck on our own expectations, feelings and ideas; when the reality doesn't match that, we don't always take it very well. Such a simple exercise acts as a reminder of everyone's good intentions and the role they all have to play.

**How to infuse a boost for better?**

The described symptoms occur when individually we narrow and close our minds to the thoughts of *I*. How we react to criticism, to friction, to fear, to others' actions… We need to foster an environment that flips the coin, one where the emotional intelligence of individuals and teams is fostered, developing an open mindset beyond ourselves. Opening our minds to the thoughts of *We*.

This idea of an open mindset reminds me of the work of Carol Dweck on the "Fixed and Growth Mindset".[73] These studies are based on education, and the idea that students who believe

---

72      Norman L. Kerth, *Project Retrospectives: A Handbook for Team Reviews* (New York: Dorset House Publishing Co., 2001)

73      Stanford Alumni, *Developing a Growth Mindset with Carol Dweck*, YouTube, www.youtube.com/watch?v=hiiEeMN-7vbQ

in their own potential for progress do better than those who believe their horizons are limited. The key is to embrace the concept of "yet".

Being part of something meaningful opens up possibilities. As humans, we have the need to contribute beyond our immediate self. We pursue contributions greater than ourselves.

That is, in fact, what organisations can offer.

Rather than introducing perks such as free smoothie bars and corporate gig nights—which are missing the point—invest in having and conveying a vision worth contributing to.

Through being involved with Pledge 1%[74]—which I will encourage you to check and be part of—I've learned about the efforts of DocuSign[75]. Their core goal is to digitise documents, and since 2003 they have helped organisations to replace over 20 billion sheets of paper with digital processes instead, which translates to a preservation of over 2.5 million trees. That's their core.

What will you do today, at the heart of your operations, that can be the organic extension to strive for better?

Find your core—you don't have to reinvent the wheel. They extended their commitments through the initiative of DocuSign IMPACT, where the "employees have volunteered thousands of hours at organisations promoting healthier forests, including urban forests in the communities where we work and live." As well as encouraging volunteering, they have donated USD 2.5 million to organisations such as The Wilderness Society, Rainforest Trust, The Nature Conservancy and Trees for Cities. Preserving the world's forests, all in line with their core.

---

74      *Pledge 1 Percent*, www.pledge1percent.org

75      *Let's agree to protect the world's forests,* DocuSign, www.docusign.co.uk/forests

Find your core where investment results in wider value, from expertise, materials, processes, networks, etc. So start from within—I bet many of your employees have already expressed interest in getting involved with sustainability efforts. You can gauge interest and potential ideas simply by sending a company-wide poll to brainstorm ways for your company to get involved in protecting the planet.

What is the uniqueness of your company that you can position to offer? Leverage your existing talent and assets, then you can initiate boost mode.

### The ripples on societal well-being

The tweaks and adjustments that we make, have a ripple effect in our extended circle of influence.

I'd like to refer back to Ørsted, and their offshore wind program in Grimsby, an English seaport town that has suffered a post-industrial decline. Ørsted appeared on the scene when its first office opened in 2014, including a GBP 10 million extension to their East Coast Hub operations and maintenance facility. This has helped breathe new life into the dockside; the site now being the world's largest offshore wind operations and maintenance centre.

Offshore wind has already boosted the local economy and, by producing renewable energy, helped transform the town. From 25 employees 6 years ago, to +350 and growing, all which have been encouraged to be part of the development and growth around the Grimsby area. At the same time, they are balancing their work-life equation with many living within an hour's distance of the site.

What you do in one area has spillovers beyond it, and it is a great example of how a core activity can lead to an economic recovery for a whole area. An area which now depends on it fundamentally, including the town's small stores, shops, restaurants and fishermen. Will Douglas, the Director of Dock Beers remarked that "10 years ago it was not possible to run a brewery company in Grimsby, but now a lot of people are spending time having drinks there, meanwhile the whole city's infrastructure is facing a great retrofit."[76]

At the core of what you do, you can in fact create positive inertia which can have a snowball effect beyond your organisation's virtual boundaries. For example, Docusign have regionally organised teams who work to identify and develop opportunities at a local level to reduce the organisation's footprint and influence leaner operations. As a couple of examples of their influence, they help to make purchasing decisions or establish partner efforts and tree-planting events. This ethos exists right at the centre of what they do. Even as an extension on their products; by featuring a "paper-impact calculator" alongside their products, customers are helped to estimate their wood, water, waste, and carbon savings resulting from reduced paper use. The calculator is powered by the Environmental Paper Network, an environmental nonprofit whose mission is to promote more sustainable paper consumption and production.[77]

You don't have to do this alone. It's not a one-time effort, nor one-directional.

## Regeneration by design

We mentioned the work of John Fullerton on this subject. How can we extrapolate this concept from nature to our organisations to infuse resilience?

Regeneration is a concept from biology that explains the process of renewal, restoration and tissue growth that makes genomes, cells, organisms and ecosystems resilient to natural fluctuations

---

76      Ørsted - World's most sustainable energy company, *Off-shore wind is transforming Grimsby: Turning the Tide (mini documentary),* YouTube, www.youtube.com/watch?v=I2ewKOGBihw

77      *Paper Calculator,* Environmental Paper Network, https://c.environmentalpaper.org/

or events that cause disturbance or damage.[78] Every species is capable of regeneration, from bacteria to human beings.

How can we apply systems thinking to our operating system architecture, to be regenerative by design? Start by looking at things to understand the underlying dynamics, so that they become better at constant fluctuations—which are characteristic of life.

Take the idea of multicellular organisms having the ability to repair and maintain integrity. How could this apply to your operations? Look at your visual circular flow of value. What are your abilities to self-restore? And what is the time in doing so for each segment?

In terms of regeneration in nature, we can also learn about the concept of autotomy, and apply it to our systems architecture. An example of this phenomenon in nature is when animals detach a tail as a defensive mechanism. Observing this phenomenon we can see that it should be easy—encouraged even—to abandon something when it no longer serves its purpose: discarding those parts which are unnecessary or even detrimental could actually sustain your wider organisation. When any one part becomes obsolete, you can replace that element with minimal fuss.

> *"You don't scale a complex system by aggregation or imitation but by decomposition to an optimal level of granularity followed by recombination...in context"* [79]

> Dave Snowden

---

78      *Regeneration,* Wikipedia, ww.en.wikipedia.org/wiki/Regeneration_(biology)

79      Dave Snowden, *Scaling in complex systems,* Cognitive Edge, https://www.cognitive-edge.com/scaling-in-complex-systems/

A system performs to fulfil the role that it was designed for. The process may be broken, not the individuals within. How can you embed regeneration so that the entirety can be rapidly restored?

Building upon that collective life-cycle picture, there may be areas that aptly represent a conundrum of letting go *for survival*. And I'm not talking here about the people and capabilities, but of *attempts of value*. With 'attempts of value' I refer to when an effort is not yielding as it was hoped for, drop the attempt not the skills. Before going gung-ho, you need to answer this question and answer it well: How can dropping a business idea be done without emotional or financial pain from all parties involved? Explore possibilities asking "What if?"

And that's where you start your regeneration by design.

Ask yourself today, where are you favouring options that have proven safe? That is where you are slowing yourself down. Shift your mindset to instead create safe spaces in which to experiment and fail is part of the process.

> *"Systems need to be managed not only for productivity or stability, they also need to be managed for resilience—the ability to recover from perturbation, the ability to restore or repair themselves."*[80]
>
> Donella H. Meadows

Most organisations still haven't fully grasped the urgent need to set an atmosphere of resilience, one which is open to others' suggestions and ideas, where it is easy to network and work towards the common goal—without doing this, they are missing out.

There is one conceptually simple thing that you can start infusing today, to boost morale, energy and effectiveness—

---

80      Donella H. Meadows, *Thinking In Systems: A Primer* (White River Junction: Chelsea Green Publishing, 2008)

praise and express gratitude. Yet, it is something that we often hold back from doing, why? That's what Erica Boothby, Xuan Zhao and Vanessa K. Bohns set themselves to answer. They found that anxiety and pessimism "causes them to refrain from engaging in this behavior that would make everyone better off."[81] For that boost behaviour that would make everyone better off, you can start with yourself and practise what you preach—whether it is giving compliments or expressing gratitude, whilst within context, sincere and being specific. It lifts moods, and contributes to positive well-being in the workplace—that is for both givers and receivers.

81      Erica Boothby, Xuan Zhao, and Vanessa K. Bohns, *A Simple Compliment Can Make a Big Difference,* Harvard Business Review, https://hbr.org/2021/02/a-simple-compliment-can-make-a-big-difference

# C is for Co-create

From the effort you've now put in to depict your current operating system of flow—including the life-cycle across your value chain—you are naturally finding your bottlenecks and production of waste.

> *"What's happening isn't an averaging out of the fluctuations in our various speeds, but an accumulation of the fluctuations. And mostly it's an accumulation of slowness—because dependency limits the opportunities for higher fluctuations. And that's why the line is spreading."*[82]
>
> Eliyahu M. Goldratt

You can't fix that alone. As the saying goes: if you want to go fast, go alone; if you want to go far, go together.

Although I'm using concepts from manufacturing, we need to be careful with some connotations. The industrial revolution also brought about thinking of people as resources—a viewpoint which has detrimental effects. Back then, we focused more on execution than innovation. Organisations are operating systems of humans, each one unique; that is an advantage. Thinking of someone as nothing more than a cog in a machine is rude, shortsighted and bad for business.

---

82    Eliyahu M. Goldratt, *What is this thing called Theory of Constraints and how should it be implemented?* (Great Barrington: North River Press, 1990)

We must move our operating systems away from directing the work of others by doing and controlling. Instead we must move towards enabling; liberating creativity and holding ourselves accountable to the results we have committed to—not we have had imposed upon us.

When thinking about crafting a system that is regenerative by design, look for silos. "Going solo" doesn't support a system structure that can regenerate and it's not sustainable either. I often observe in organisations that speed—regardless of how big or small the item at hand is—without self-imposed control becomes reckless.

*"There's more to life than increasing its speed."*[83]

Mohandas K. Gandhi

And that's coming from me, an Agile Coach; I help organisations and teams to deliver better value sooner. Sooner is important. Sooner enables you to go to market earlier, which is a key competitive advantage. Yet, just going *fast* and doing so in silos does not support or generate any advantage—it can't be sustained over time, it doesn't scale and lacks enrichment.

What we often face is a very deep attachment to our own ideas, which without perspective in turn drives private agendas and generates silos. Another driver is the sense of being in a constant hurry and racing against the clock, getting things done just *fast* has its implications such as patches and unscalable solutions. There is always more than one way to look at something, what you want is to enrich options, not to polarise them.

Look for diverse teams, foster and build upon each other's ideas and perspectives. That comes with the added bonus

---

83     Mohandas K. Gandhi as quoted by Susan Ratcliffe in *Oxford Essential Quotations, 5 ed.* (Oxford: Oxford University Press, 2017)

of building networks, interconnectedness and institutional knowledge across your organisation. Your operating system.

To be able to co-create in your organisation, you need to connect information and relationships, both to be driven by transparency and fairness, focus on learning and what is achieved—rather than just what it's been done. For co-create to exist it requires distributed control and autonomy, guided by clear purpose, have a shared common challenge across the distributed control and be based on an inspiring and cohesive bigger picture.

## A sample of co-creation enablement

In 2009, a sustainable fashion brand was born, Ecoalf.[84] With an initial investment of EUR 2 million in 2012, it has had huge rates of growth and is expected to achieve EUR 24 million by 2021.

Today, across 11 countries, Ecoalf manages the full process from waste collection to recycling technologies, manufacture, design and retail. They are reducing carbon emissions by using renewable energy in their stores and headquarters. In addition, they implemented a "circular design" strategy that includes design with the end of life of the product in mind: low impact materials selection, timeless and essential design with less material and fewer processes, to reduce the impact in the value chain. With a focus on high quality and durability, to maximise the product life cycle.

Ecoalf works closely with its suppliers, helping them to improve their processes and energy efficiency and integrate the most innovative and efficient ones. Javier Goyeneche, the founder of Ecoalf, spent the first three years sourcing and developing fabrics. The problem they faced was that the range of recycled materials on offer was small and of very poor quality. Most fabrics contained only a small percentage of recycled material

---

84      *Ecoalf*, Ecoalf, www.ecoalf.com

(15-20%), so he found the need to start creating partnerships with factories in order to develop fabrics, lining, straps, labels and cords using recycled materials.

The goal was to create the first generation of recycled products with the same quality, design and technical properties as the best non-recycled products, to show that there is no need to use our world's natural resources in a careless way. Their materials are made from discarded fishing nets, post-consumer plastic bottles, worn-out tires, post-industrial cotton and used coffee grounds.

As you can imagine, when Ecoalf first emerged another big challenge came to the surface: how to change people's conceptual approach to recycling—as recycling and quality did not seem to connect. Ecoalf's efforts during the past years have proven that in fact, recycling connects with quality and design. Their efforts and statements have resulted in a change of mentality for their customer base; people now believe that pre-used items are natural resources—the same quality can be attained.

Goyeneche believes the finite earth material utilisation mindset change can not be driven solely by governments, it also needs to be done by any size company, including smaller companies. Organisations are to become the ones who will guide the customer towards this world where we are all focused on recycling and sustainability, and demonstrate that things can be done differently.

Goyeneche had spent a year investigating the feasibility of the project and finding all the right partners, such as recycling facilities, spinners, weavers and most importantly Fishermen Associations. Yes, fishing. That's because every day, fishermen are pulling up a huge amount of plastic from their nets and the most common industry practice is to just throw it right back in the sea.

Today, Ecoalf has 11 active alliances around the world: Taiwan, Korea, Portugal, Mexico, Japan, Spain, etc. These alliances allow them to continually develop all the necessary elements to be able to manufacture with recycled materials. Ecoalf also relies on 14 joint ventures to collect waste from the oceans and coasts of the Mediterranean.

This is known as Deep Democracy—the "belief in the inherent importance of all parts of ourselves and all viewpoints in the world around us". Co-creation enablement within your organisation and across your whole value chain.

For example, as a certified B-Corp since March 2018, Ecoalf is legally required to consider the impact of their decisions on their workers, customers, suppliers, community and the environment.[85] It is also worth noting that they were the first organisation in Spain to attain the B-Corp certification.

It's rather inspiring and eye-opening when we consider how they have been able to connect information and relationships to their mission.

**Infuse, Inspire and Ignite your surroundings**

How can you get others involved as a core part of the solution? Not just your circle of influence, but also your community and beyond?

People want to be part of value-driven organisations, where one can have an impact in areas that one is passionate about.

One of the concepts that deeply resonated with me, from Kate Raworth's work, is the entity often overlooked: *the commons.* "Natural commons have traditionally emerged in communities seeking to steward Earth's 'common pool' resources, such as grazing land, fisheries, watersheds and forests. Cultural commons serve to keep alive a community's language, heritage and rituals, myths and music, traditional knowledge and

---

85      *Ecoalf recycled fabrics,* B Corporation, www.bcorpora-tion.eu/directory/ecoalf-recycled-fabrics-sl

practice. And the fast-growing digital commons are stewarded collaboratively online, co-creating open-source software, social networks, information and knowledge."[86] Which are creative therefore we should unleash their potential.

What are your context, your mission and your surroundings? What are the commons that you may be tapping into and how are you doing so?

For Javier Goyeneche, Founder and President of Ecoalf, the mission started to emerge after speaking with a fisherman— who showed him the amount of plastic caught in fishermen's nets. It was this that brought home a realisation which turned into Upcycling the Oceanseffort—"a worldwide adventure that will help remove marine debris from the bottom of the oceans thanks to the support of certain fishermen."[87] Together with Nacho Llorca, President of the Association of Fishermen of Levante, they started an ocean clean-up project.[88] In 2018, with about 2,500 fishermen collaborating, it started there in Levante Port in Spain and as a result, that year they were taking out around 280 tonnes of garbage from the oceans surrounding all of Spain.

---

86      Kate Raworth, *Doughnut Economics: Seven Ways to Think Like a 21st-Century Economist* (New York: Random House, 2018)

87      *Upcycling The Oceans,* Ecoalf, www.ecoalf.com/es/p/up-cycling-the-oceans-15

88      Ecoalf, *Ecoalf x Brightvibes UTO España,* YouTube, www.youtube.com/watch?v=q1NNJ-dBAp0&feature=youtu.be

| Result | 2015 | 2016 | 2017 | 2018 | 2019 | 2020 |
|---|---|---|---|---|---|---|
| ● Total Waste (T) | 23 | 54 | 113 | 140 | 152 | 180 |
| ● Ports | 9 | 9 | 32 | 37 | 40 | 40 |
| ● Boats | 165 | 165 | 462 | 546 | 550 | 573 |
| ▨ Fishermen | 743 | 743 | 2079 | 2534 | 2600 | 2575 |

89

*Figure 2.2: Upcycling The Oceans initiative Ecoalf results table from 2015 to 2020 (Ports, Boats and Fishermen involved and total waste collected)*

Figure 2.2 illustrates the total waste collected each year from 2015 to 2020, from ports, boats and fishermen. The number of fishermen involved increased from 743 in 2015 to 2575 in 2020; this resulted in the total tonnes of waste collected increasing from 23 to 180 tonnes in that period. Since 2015, they have been running a similar project in Thailand. Their first official event took place in Koh Samed island in 2017, with 100 divers and 300 volunteers. After 5 hours, a total of 0.7 tonnes of marine waste was collected. The year after, 900 volunteers recovered 0.85 tonnes of waste.

Through the Mediterranean Clean Up project, they support Enaleia in sorting the waste in six Greek ports with 35 boats and more than 200 fishermen involved. During the last fishing period, they got 10 fishing boats involved to work in this program, and cleaned a total of 16 tonnes of marine litter, of which 83% was plastic. In fact, the UN Environment Program selected this program among the Top 5 best initiatives in Europe for 2019 for its positive impact on the environment.

Whilst talking about this initiative, Nacho emphasises they alone cannot solve the problem by cleaning up the ocean, they need people to focus on the source of the problem—reduce

89      *Upcycling The Oceans,* Ecoalf, www.ecoalf.com/en/p/upcycling-the-oceans-spain-16

waste on Earth. Javier points out that fishermen are doing this for free, during the 12-hour shift that they spend on the ocean fishing. This brings to light that each one of us can take personal action now in whatever we do, without too much extra effort, to help to heal our planet and for it to be a better place to live in.

Collaboration and co-creation are competitive advantages, because doing so you infuse your efforts with varied strengths and perspectives, and that enriches the matter at hand. Diversity boosts your mission.

**How to infuse diversity?**

One quick analysis test that you can run right now is to look around your organisation. Does it mirror your pool of customers? Is your organisation, department, team etc. a representative voice? Is that voice resonating with a wider audience?

McKinsey researchers, in 2015 and 2018, found that companies in the top quartile for diverse leadership teams outperformed less diverse peers on profitability.[90] Stalled progress on diversity makes it even more difficult as time passes, just like technical debt. Stalled progress on diversity may also result in a negative perception of your brand among customers, current employees, potential talent and investors who increasingly view diversity as the basis of a well-functioning environment.

---

90        Sundiatu Dixon-Fyle, Kevin Dolan, Vivian Hunt, and Sara Prince, *Diversity Wins: How inclusion matters,* McKinsey & Company, www.mckinsey.com/featured-insights/diversi-ty-and-inclusion/diversity-wins-how-inclusion-matters

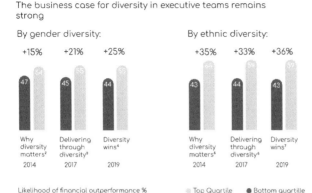

The business case for diversity in executive teams remains strong

By gender diversity:

+15%   +21%   +25%

| Why diversity matters[2] | Delivering through diversity[3] | Diversity wins[4] |
| 2014 | 2017 | 2019 |

By ethnic diversity:

+35%   +33%   +36%

| Why diversity matters[5] | Delivering through diversity[6] | Diversity wins[7] |
| 2014 | 2017 | 2019 |

Likelihood of financial outperformance %   ⬤ Top Quartile   ⬤ Bottom quartille

Likelihood of financial outperformance vs the national industry median; p-value <0.05, except 2014 data where p-value <0.1. [2]n = 383; Latin America, UK, and US; earnings before interest and taxes (EBIT) margin 2010-13. [3]n = 991; Australia, Brazil, France, Germany, India, Japan, Mexico, Nigeria, Singapore, South Africa, UK, and US ; EBIT margin 2011-15. [4]n = 1,039; 2017 companies for which gender data available in 2019, plus Denmark, Norway, and Sweden; EBIT margin 2014-18. [5]n = 364; Latin America, UK, and US; EBIT margin 2010-13. [6]n = 589; Brazil, Mexico, Singapore, South Africa, UK, and US; EBIT margin 2011-15. [7]n = 533; Brazil, Mexico, Nigeria, Singapore, South Africa, UK, and US, where ethnicity data available in 2019; EBIT margin 2014-18. Source: Diversity Wins data set

*Figure 2.3: The business case for diversity in executive teams remains strong. Vertical graphs on gender and ethnic diversity. Adapted from McKinsey diversity-and-inclusion.*

The graph in Figure 2.3 shows the likelihood of financial outperformance for 2014, 2017 and 2019. Each section shows the difference between the bottom and top quartiles by gender diversity on the left and ethnic diversity on the right. When measured by gender diversity, the percentage differences between the top and bottom quartiles are 15% for 'Why diversity matters' in 2014, 21% for 'Delivering through diversity' in 2017, and 25% for 'Diversity wins' in 2019. For ethnic diversity, the percentage differences are 35% for 'Why diversity matters' in 2014, 33% for 'Delivering through diversity' in 2017, and 36% for 'Diversity wins' in 2019.

The fruit of diversity is collective creativity, reaching new highs, an enriched perspective and a boost of entrepreneurial energy. It needs to become a constant reinforcing loop in your system. It's just so easy to fall into old habits, our own silos of reality, segregation and polarisation of ideas, our own bias, and a loss of sight.

As an antidote, you can embed diversity in your strategy and operations in the following ways:

- Ensure diverse talent representation at all levels
- Gather data and make it available on demand
- Clearly define goals
- Hold leaders accountable on progress
- Have a simple, transparent, equal and fair system of opportunities
- Talent pool to be circular and regenerative by design
- Train everyone on awareness and behaviour, as well as how to escalate issues
- Snap out of existence microaggressions early, simply, unpainfully

It's a journey rather than a destination. And it goes beyond gender and ethnicity.

Last year I came across a model of a diversity map; it accounted for how we relate and connect, how we think and process information, what we believe and feel, what we do professionally and also how we do it, physical traits and many others. A model which unfortunately I haven't been able to locate again. Diversity is wide, it promotes health, vitality, productivity of ecosystems; just like in nature.

The urge to affiliate with others is innate. We are, after all, interconnected. We may be distributed, but that does not mean we are dispersed. To co-create a system that as a whole is greater than the simple sum of its parts, we need a system which includes quality in its interactions.

This includes the mindful design of the system map. For example, do not decouple an "innovation hub" from the rest; instead a regenerative system should have innovation embedded throughout. Separating it as its own entity removes the responsibility from the rest, it alienates it from your flow and restricts the ability to co-create. You see this often in technology teams which separate the *creation* and *maintenance* of those creations; separate environments, separate operations, separate information feedback flows. All this separation leads inevitably to disparate outcomes.

Co-creating is about having a high level of cooperation, sharing risks and ideas, learning and spreading the acquired wisdom quickly, supporting and challenging each other, and thriving for better as a standard state of affairs... it becomes the connective tissue within your organisation.

For it to naturally happen, you need organic safety as we mentioned, a sense of belonging, and the ability for all individuals involved to have personal significance. Safety that is not forced, that is expected and is nurtured. Belonging is a fundamental part of the group, the mission, the vision. And place significance on the individual value each one brings to the whole.

You may have heard of the Portland aviation crash in 1978.[91] The disaster that killed 10 people became a pivotal moment for the aviation industry, which radically changed how crews got trained. This crash taught the world the repercussions of fixation and unchallenged lines of command—how these can easily lead to disasters. Employees are not there to simply obey and shut up! Employees at all levels are stakeholders who are (or should be) invested in the value and impact of the organisation. Whether you're the CEO or the newest intern that's your role, your duty and why you were hired.

---

91      National Transportation Safety Board, *Aircraft Accident Report,* Media Oregon Live, https://media.oregonlive.com/history/other/2014/12/28/NTSB%20investigation.pdf

Instead of the focus on lines of command, the emphasis must be on teamwork, on crafting multiple open paths of communication, on support and cooperation, on the importance of listening and speaking one's mind, on what's often called social intelligence—through which we can learn from others' successes and failures.

**Leverage connections**

Doing so comes down to being yourself and using your judgement. The more connected people are at work, the more synched they are, the more this leads to being happier and more effective.

Deliberately generate a space which enables those connections to happen. You can't force it, but you can influence it. Which opportunities are you creating?

How people land—either as a brand new addition to the organisation or in a new position, department etc.—has a big influence on what comes next. One of the things I have been experimenting with in teams over the last couple of years is the concept of a buddy system. It's totally borrowed from scuba diving—where two divers with similar interests share a dive— that connection being a supporting mechanism and more long-lasting. Imagine an organisation where everyone has a buddy to go through the motions when landing together. As in scuba diving, even though each and everyone is in charge of their own *oxygen and equipment*—you remain within distance, keeping on-hand and providing an extra perspective.

Another experiment that has worked well for many teams is having an all day meeting link. Fairly practical and simple. That link is an enabler, a virtual room available during working hours—all-day every-day—that people can join at any point. It's multipurpose really, it serves to: ask questions, have a virtual coffee, a team lunch and bounce ideas off each other. Always using the same link makes it easy and accessible, no matter who might want to use it or what they may want to use it for.

You may observe that the use of a virtual drop-in space will come and go in waves starting as a novelty with more attention, becoming quieter in oscillations, then picking up throughout different delivery times… and that's okay. It's there as and when needed—a space for the team, led by the team. Even in a recent organisation that I have been working with, this practice has been used by some team members as a silent space for people to work remotely, in silence together. Whatever works really.

What other opportunities for connections can you create? With the shift to virtual—which for some almost happened overnight in 2020—casual conversations that may have happened in corridors or at the tea station are no longer there. How can you enable, naturally, non-forced, that goodness to have a chance to happen in a remote environment? Distributed not dispersed.

Size does matter: the previously mentioned study by Woohoo Inc. showed that 36% of people in workplaces with 1-10 employees report having a good work day every day or almost every day. I'm not surprised that smaller work groups have more good days, not to necessarily say that big corporations fail in this arena, but there is something about cooperatives, horizontals, fractal organisations, self-organised teams that really allow employees to connect to leverage relationships, partnerships and co-creation.

Working in smaller *bundles* does enable more effective decision making, that decision making and commitment to a greater whole being at its lowest possible levels. Think about fractal organisations, where members share information and make decisions collectively as conditions change, forming a network of capabilities. Organic on-demand coordination as a mutual understanding component with a common purpose.

# Call. Be. Act.

*"There is no wealth but life...That country is the richest which nourishes the greatest number of noble and happy human beings"[92]*

John Ruskin

Good health is at the centre of well-being, and it's vital for everything we care for; so that we can learn, thrive, and be productive. We must aim for the highest possible goals. Having this attitude has a direct impact on what you may be measuring today; look at the intangible asset off your balance sheet—named under human capital. Small gains on well-being have huge gains for your organisation. Including your own well-being. This has synergy and it's bi-directional.

Time for a wrap-up of our Happy ABCs—Acknowledge, Boost and Co-create. Actions that you can start today:

**Measure your well-being health**

Run this tiny calculator fridaypulse.com/calculator or Heartcount.com. And at a personal level check fridayone.com happiness calculator.

---

92      John Ruskin, *Unto This Last* (London: Penguin Classics, 1985)

Even if you just start with a simple assessment of your state of affairs, you can get an initial sense of your progress towards the 5 factors that Woohoo Inc found cause a good day at work:

- Is the work I do meaningful? And positively affected someone else?

- Do I have freedom to work my own way whilst supporting others?

- Do I do work that I am proud of?

- Do I have fun with my peers?

- Do I find the tasks I do enjoyable?

Infuse it with the three applications of emotional intelligence. So that you can find out if people are:

- Able to air grievances as helpful critiques

- Working in an atmosphere in which diversity is valued (not a source of friction)

- Able to network effectively

Do diagnose this by looking at actual vs perceived. Account for your workplace history, geopolitics, culture and inner economy.

**Craft your mission; start within**

Rather than wait for some magic formula for a top-down reform, how can you self-organise in ranged networks to drive—at micro level—the changes and support that you wish to see for the whole?

Gauge interest and gather potential ideas related to your core. The reality is that you do already have caring fans: colleagues, customers, shareholders/investors, community, etc—after all, an organisation is a community space maker.

**Encourage cooperative societies**

Do so beyond your team, department and organisational "walls", to extend to the ecosystem. For example, go to uplink. weforum.org/uplink, where you can propose a smart solution and then they will connect you with other entrepreneurs and investors to make an impact. You can also leverage:

- ME Climate Hub for small and medium-sized enterprises (SMEs) smeclimatehub.org
- the European Sustainable Business Hub www. clustercollaboration.eu/cluster-organisations/ sustainable-business-hub
- Innovation Warehouse innovationwarehouse.org/ sustainability-hub

And participate in advocating for existing campaigns that matter to your workforce. Also, join the movement and take the pledge1percent.org.

**Embed into the fabric**

Rather than creating a separate employee experience and diversity program, embed it in your operations and strategy as one more variable to measure and improve.

To be an amplifier of equality, you need to do that with detailed and tangible actions on the following areas:

- Education
- Training
- Exposure
- Opportunity
- Access
- Practice

The lack of the above factors often surfaces as a bottleneck in your systems flows.

**Measure it!**

Attention drives results, define the collective goals and score what matters:

- Employee representation
- Leadership diversity
- Ethical duty based on societal impact (not shares)
- Gap between more and less advantaged groups
- Directors' alignment on common goal

In addition, what is your social mobility?[93] By this I mean the actual movement of an individual's status in your organisation, not merely the perception of what is possible.

**Beware of the External God Complex**

Over the years I've come to believe that in organisations, departments, teams and even at an individual level, we suffer from what I call an *External God Complex*. A side spin of the traditional God Complex[94]—which outlines how, however difficult a problem may be, you have an overwhelming belief that you are flawlessly right—The External God Complex is the deep belief that the answers are elsewhere, that you need a perfect, magical, extensively experienced hero, application, technology, that you do not possess, and that that exists elsewhere. The deep belief that the only *way out* is for it to come and save you from all your troubles.

Be aware of the world that's around us; you do have the talent and the problem solvers to build upon each other's ideas, to experiment and learn. So lift others as you rise.

---

93      *Social mobility,* Wikipedia, www.en.wikipedia.org/wiki/Social_mobility

94      *God complex,* Wikipedia, https://en.wikipedia.org/wiki/God_complex

## Create an antipattern recipe

Foster an environment for your innovators to meet, partner and experiment. Do that with confidence and mastery, curiosity and interest in understanding and being understood, continuance and resilience, capacity and the wish to have an impact, cooperate and communicate, to balance one's own needs with others. Give yourself permission to start giving sincere and specific compliments multiple times a day.

Do all of this by co-creating, to enrich a better acknowledgement of where you are now and where you are heading. Problem solving and collaboration are learnable skills so that one can stay connected.

# Part Three

# Profit

L ast but not least, Profit. We could summarise the chapter with this simple phrase:

Profit is the <u>result</u> of the two previous parts.

After all, we need to be economically viable to be *in the game*. Yet, via sustainability and happiness we are able to make it a better game.

> *"...success isn't about how much money you make, it's about the difference you make in people's lives."*[95]
>
> Michelle Obama

I argue that profits are a by-product. A result of thinking responsibly—about employees, gains, tax contribution, the ones we serve, the environment and society—rather than just tactically. Profits may be a condition to be *in the game* but are not the goal.

It starts with why. We need a purpose that is more than just maximising returns—and that "more" lasts. A purpose to create long term value, where gains are fairly distributed and where we leave the place better than how we found it. If you

95        Michelle    Obama,    *Transcript:    Michelle Obama's    Convention    Speech,*    NPR,    https://www.npr.org/2012/09/04/160578836/transcript-michelle-obamas-convention-speech?t=1627029997247

haven't yet geared towards this direction, then bluntly put: you are late.

Don't panic, the first thing you can do is be open to optimising how your value flows through the system as a priority over focusing on assets. We tend to look at assets as a reduction of profit to the bottom line. Instead, focus the efforts in your flow towards becoming a lean organisation that delivers value, with deeply engaged and caring fans—this is what generates profit.

We need to realise and acknowledge that, over the years, we have become obsessed with growth. We hear and talk about growth over profit and value. Growth per se—as any silo metric—misses the wider reality lens. For example, you can aim to increase your customer numbers; firstly, that does not account for the limit available and secondly, just having more does not make one successful. And growth is not a limitless entity either.

As a useful model to account for that idea of limits to what is available, we could look at the Maximum Sustainable Yield concept.[96] This is used to calculate, as an example, the largest catch in fisheries that can be taken from a stock over an indefinite period. Another model to keep in mind is the Gaia Paradigm, which outlines how living organisms and inorganic surroundings form synergistic and self-regulating complex systems which maintain conditions for life on the planet.[97] Unless one manages in a sustainable manner, one collapses. Growth is not an endless entity.

Our economic world is a human invention, with the intention to organise ourselves in big numbers. How can we expect it to

---

96    *Maximum sustainable yield,* Wikipedia, www.en.wikipedia.org/wiki/Maximum_sustainable_yield

97    *Gaia hypothesis,* Wikipedia, www.en.wikipedia.org/wiki/Gaia_hypothesis

grow endlessly, when in fact the Earth is finite? We do have planetary boundaries, nine in fact:[98]

- Climate change
- Ocean acidification
- Ozone depletion
- Nitrogen and phosphorus levels
- Freshwater depletion
- Extinction and biodiversity loss
- Land system change
- Chemical pollution
- Atmospheric aerosol loading

Thanks to the work of Johan Rockström from the Stockholm Resilience Centre and Will Steffen from the Australian National University, we have a structure to measure what is the safe operating space for humanity and quantify where we are in each dimension. In the case of at least four climate change, biodiversity loss, land-system change, nitrogen and phosphorus levels we are already operating in the high-risk zone.

As the economic world is invented, we can reshape it and come up with something better. There is not a question anymore of economic growth with some environmental reduction, but a question to frame the model so that it actually serves us. Let's develop an economic world in a different way—to its very core—so that we can reconcile *growth* with what we want to see in the ecological realities and humanity's well-being.

If our ultimate responsibility is to maximise profits, what change of model do we need to make? A model that enables us not just to be within the boundaries, but to regenerate them?

---

98     *Planetary boundaries,* Wikipedia, https://en.wikipedia.org/wiki/Planetary_boundaries

You may be under the impression that you have what works on returns as it is, have you really looked?

At governmental level there has been—and still is—much discussion on the subject of growth, and over the last few years there has been higher consciousness at the mass individual level. However, I believe we haven't really grasped the extent of our troubles and the detrimental impact that our operations have had, and continue to have. For the most part, we don't realise the consequences of our acts, there is an information feedback loop missing and the majority of the repercussions have not yet surfaced as there is a big feedback delay.

Many individuals, companies and countries around the world have made a commitment to being carbon neutral. This means taking action to reduce their GHG emissions to zero—and then 'offsetting' an equivalent amount of any remaining emissions. The terms 'net zero emissions' and 'carbon neutrality' are interchangeable; the core meaning of both is the understanding of the need to achieve ecological balance between the activities that emit climate pollution and the processes that reduce the impact of that pollution to zero, or close to zero. Both terms require a phase-out of fossil fuel emissions, hand in hand with a phase-in of energy efficiency and renewable energy—both phases complemented by measures to bring down emissions from agriculture and forestry, to achieve overall ecological balance.

Whilst many organisations are waking up to the idea of achieving carbon neutrality, you have the opportunity to set yourself apart from others by becoming a carbon sink. Meaning you reduce more emissions than you pollute—your climate-protecting efforts more than make up for your emissions, rendering you an active cleanser of the planet as opposed to just a "do no harm" player.

As covered in Part One, sustainability is not a nice-to-have—as business leaders we must recognise that doing nothing isn't an option. Doing nothing isn't a smart strategy to reduce GHG emissions. Doing nothing doesn't help us in any way to become a lean organisation with deeply engaged and caring fans.

We are to do our fair share, including within our ecosystem. How does one decide who to partner with in this journey? How can we craft those partnerships? How can we position ourselves?

The current state of affairs with respect to the nine planetary boundaries is not a pretty picture—we do need to go beyond *mission zero*. Meaning, becoming an organisation with products, services, buildings and assets driving our business with zero environmental impact is not good enough to solve the situation we have put ourselves in. We need to generate surplus.

We can replenish the living world and the communities that we are here to serve. The concept of regenerative enterprise means that we leave things in a better state than how we found them.

The thing is we can't afford to wait to act. $CO_2$ emissions stay in the atmosphere for decades (if not centuries). So even if we had the ability to turn off an imaginary switch right now—we will still see in the days, months and years to come increased repercussions from emissions that we have already released into the atmosphere. We are unable to see yet because of the feedback delay.

The good news is that we can, of course, reduce our $CO_2$ emissions whilst still being a profitable business. This can be achieved in many ways, to start by utilising the perspective of resource saving technologies and by shifting energy away from fossil fuels.

In addition, start to think about taxation—there are on the way discussions about what is coming down the line, from covering taxes for GHG emissions, paid pollution volume permits, the increase of costs to the pollutants etc. So rather than wait, be smarter and act beforehand—be on the leading edge and become a regenerative organisation.

Economically speaking it's in our own interest, as we mentioned there are taxations and increases in costs coming up. Also, the repercussions of the depletion of certain fuel and resources, which in turn makes those more costly and become non viable in many ways.

The increase of social awareness on the subject has also a direct impact on your brand perception and purchase decisions. Hence the importance of care across your whole value chain. GHG emissions affect us all globally. Shifting the same practices elsewhere on the planet—and/or not wanting to be aware of certain practices—does not make the problem go away. Nor does it take us anywhere closer to solve it.

We all breathe the same air. It is still our responsibility, how the changes we made in one part of the system affect another. There are liability rules for pollution responsibility up and downstream, and we have the ability to know where we are and change course away from harmful practices.

We should be more aware of how our decisions are detrimentally impacting the world and other people. The repercussions that have been and will be felt across generations. It's morally wrong, and therefore, we need to think differently and think ahead. From engaging with community efforts on scarce land, forest, endangered species, to tapping into social institutions that engage on such behaviours at scale.

Remember, find your core—your purpose, and, yes, then one can still be profitable.

# A is for Accelerate

One of the key elements of circular economy thinking is designing-out waste, including and especially from the product inception phase.

From inception, embedding the scientific method helps our focus to reduce waste. The scientific method basically consists of systematic observation, measurement, experimentation, formulation, testing and modification of hypotheses. Moving then from hypothesis to statements, from statements to experiments, which we observe and measure, which inform our next steps, including changes to the hypothesis itself.

In using this method we need to ensure that we consider the full range of any variable or function, so that it can help us tune and adjust towards what's really needed. Just like deltas in maths.

The constant inspection and adaptation is what enables acceleration at a rate no other method can bring. Especially in comparison to predefined linear deterministic processes. Predefined linear approaches have proven wrong over and over again, yet today are spread all over organisations for some strange reason. My take? Those predefined linear approaches give us a false sense of security, which we are unconsciously drawn to. Pretending that we are in control is not only a recipe for mistakes it also prevents us from learning from those mistakes! We must break through.

Organisations are innovative, the reason for their existence is to solve a problem that wasn't solved before or wasn't solved in that manner. One can do that with constant ideas surfacing to find new paths to fulfil that purpose.

Today's competitive advantage is basically based on two key things: The first is the speed to market with persistent experimentation, and then the second is the ability to swiftly transform some of those experimental business ideas into fully-fledged products and services.

You are measured on the value that you deliver, not on what's been done.

Look around, search for the current amount of time and effort that is put in by your team, department, organisation measuring what's done and what's in progress, rather than focusing on the value delivered. Look at the repercussions of this focus: from context switch and distractions, shift away from delivering value, living in the past to slowing you down. Has what has been done, brought value?

The second item that prevents us from accelerating is the amount of time and effort invested (I'd argue, mostly wasted) on selection and prioritisation. Think about it, how many months are currently spent attempting to agree on next year's business priorities? As part of that process compromises are inevitable. Therefore, even after all those months, meetings and effort, we end up with an inaccurate and mediocre list.

I'd like to present you with another lens to look through: impact. Invest time, effort, focus and intelligence into assessing impact. You do this by getting your ideas to market, not sitting around talking about what might happen when you do. Once they're out there, you can validate them with real-life evidence of impact! From that, you can decide whether to pivot or persevere. Let's say you want to change your checkout basket because someone has a strong gut feeling that a tweak will increase 'add-on' purchases. Sure, you can involve everyone, have loads of discussions about the design and branding of the campaign to launch, blah blah blah... Or! You can mock something up to use on a really small slice of checkouts and determine if it is in fact making the impact you want. Break free from the sunk cost fallacy!

To make space (physical and mental) for finding real impact, you need to flip the coin in two ways. One is to make experiments smaller and the second is to let go of what's consuming it from happening today, which is to remove that *in-progress status waste* and become leaner at prioritisation.

This moves you from a pull to a push system. In the technology industry, a pull system is one which is structured such that clients request data from a server periodically to check changes, so that their side server can be updated; the freshness of the data depends on the frequency of requests. The drawback of pull systems is that what often ends up happening is that clients make excessive calls and cause server slowdown. We can correlate this to what happens at a team level—what are the repercussions of a pull system where the information is held by humans, rather than machines? Where the freshness of the data depends on the request frequency? There is obviously a temptation to make frequent, if not excessive, requests for data. Now scale this to the level of department, organisation and across the whole supply chain; instead of server slowdown you have organisation slowdown.

Instead, let's think of it a bit like event trigger architecture— where the real impact value happening in the market is what drives next steps.[99]

---

99      Event trigger architecture in software development de-scribes a system where each event is generated by a change of state or previous event, e.g. a consumer may receive an emailed dis-patch notification which was generated by their product leaving the warehouse. External applications can subscribe to such events to be notified and subsequently process that change.

## Let's be smarter than our primitive inertia

Profit is, by definition, an advantage. A benefit that sets you ahead of others. That is based on the value that you bring and the effort you put into it. And yes, it includes financial efforts like the amount spent on buying, operating or producing something.

It doesn't stop there though. There are multiple long-term returns which, most often, are omitted from organisational strategies, such as human, social, ecological, cultural, physical and yes, some also financial.

A tree is known by its fruits. The worth of our products, services and organisations is determined by others based on what is produced and visible to the world. Impact is what matters. A tree's worth is not determined by how tall the tree grows; similarly our organisations are not measured on the number of employees or product lines they have. Let's not forget a tree also needs to grow its roots so that it can feed itself nutrients and hold itself up.

A great example of this is the Norway-headquartered global paper-based packaging company, Elopak. They have been a CarbonNeutral® company since 2016, whilst also delivering a range of internal emission reductions, including a 70% reduction in absolute emissions since 2008. Back in November 2018, they also committed to setting a science-based target to ensure that these internal reductions are in line with the level of decarbonisation required to keep global temperature increase below the levels advocated by the latest climate science.

One of the shifts was using renewable electricity across all of its operations. Elopak's carbon neutral goal has also been met by financing emission reduction projects that build low carbon sustainable development. Natural Capital Partners has helped them to make emissions reductions through projects that relate to their core raw material: trees. One project is Rimba Raya, which protects the rainforest and the orangutans in Borneo, Indonesia by protecting over 640 km² of rainforest from palm oil plantations. This is achieved by incentivising the local population to protect the forest and preventing illegal logging through patrols and guard towers. The project is validated and verified to the Verified Carbon Standard (VCS) and has obtained Triple Gold status within the Climate Community and Biodiversity (CCB) Standard. And since they are now supporting further projects outside of the value chain, and have split their portfolio with South Pole, in doing so they are contributing not only to reduced emissions but also facilitating positive effects on local livelihoods and the environment.

The company started in 1957 and today is a leading supplier of packaging systems for liquid food products, selling 14 billion cartons annually to 80 markets worldwide. Elopak was owned by Norway's largest privately owned industrial group, FERD Holding and in June 2021 was listed on the Oslo Stock Exchange. This huge operation's performance generates revenues of EUR 930 million per year.

They are achieving those numbers in accordance with the UN Sustainable Development Goals. Elopak is basing its efforts on four primary SDGs:[100]

- Goal 8: Decent work and economic growth.

  Right now via extending their focus of ethical practices into supply chain and skilling employees.

- Goal 12: Responsible consumption and production.

  For example their Pure-Pak® carton is fully recyclable and in line with the concept of circular economy; in this case the cartons are made from renewable sources that grow back, and are truly sustainable and recyclable materials. With a total recovery rate (recycling and energy recovery)of 76% reached in 2018.

---

100      *Sustainability Report 2019,* Elopak, www.elopak.com/wp-content/uploads/2020/09/Sustainability-Report-2019_WEB.pdf

- Goal 13: Climate Action.

  With commitment to further reduction of greenhouse emissions.

- Goal 17: Partnership for the goals.

  With the focus of working with suppliers and customers to reduce emissions and use of raw materials.

They have also outlined two SDGs as secondary goals as more of an enabler, from 15 and 14. And six more Sustainable Development Goals as indirect. All of which translates into specific targets such as:

- Offering a top-quartile motivating workplace by 2025
- Distribution of diversity across all hierarchical levels
- Key raw materials sourced through suitable value chain
- 100% recyclable beverage cartons in all markets by 2025
- 100% renewable materials available in all beverage cartons by 2030
- Active engagement in industry associations in their geographical markets

And more, all with three pillar themes behind their efforts: social responsibility from safety, employability and sourcing; environmental impact; circular economy.

**Make up your own framework**

There isn't a magic cookie cutter, model or wand that can convert your operations today. Context is everything.

For example, Elopak made up their own framework: Elovation. This is based on the vision that every employee is a problem-solver, is there to continuously improve work methods and is always adding value to their customers.

Simple, right? Elovation defines a number of principles and best practices for how they should work so that they can improve the outcome of daily tasks, whilst putting the safety of each other and the environment first.

I particularly like how it outlines the fact that each and every colleague should involve others to achieve improvements along the chain of activities. From the need to share information, to providing constant feedback not only to learn, but also to encourage the improvement of further endeavors and act as institutional knowledge. That just doesn't happen in silos.

For example, in their Fastiv plant, one of the causes of waste is polyethylene (PE) missing on the edge of the printing side of the roll fed board. To solve this, a team of people from all parts of the production line came together to find a solution to reduce waste. "The team used a problem-solving tool to ensure that the problem was commonly understood by everyone in the team. The results were formidable as waste on this particular waste cause has been reduced from 0,22% to 0,11%, all within 6 months due to a dedicated team carrying out structured problem solving with supporting tools to support them."[101]

It reminds me of the Toyota Production System, from which we learn that reducing and eliminating waste is to be the first business objective. It's all part of the art of maximising the amount of work <u>not</u> done.

Traditionally, one looks at the efficiency of capital to increase stocks and profits by growing larger. Efficiency of capital, in itself, is how much it takes to produce. You can do so more

---

101      *Sustainability Report 2019,* Elopak, www.elopak.com/wp-content/uploads/2020/07/Sustainability-Report-2019.pdf

efficiently by reducing your waste rate; cutting down what's discarded, broken and replaced.

Elopak's Elovation framework is applicable for all employees: for managers and shop-floor personnel participating in primary supply processes such as procurement, manufacturing and logistics, as well as indirectly through various support processes. Each of their plants have Elovation champions, helping them to keep continuous improvement at heart.

Every year, they also run workshops from across the different plants all around the framework. The effort of coming together yearly brings to mind the concepts we touched on of swarming and enriching each other's ideas. The action of a group jumping in together solves problems and gets things done, through self-organisation and decentralisation.

Imagine, every employee being a problem-solver with the mantra of continuously improving work methods and always adding value to customers. Breaking free of the status quo, being innovative by design.

> *"We have to get together and push with social pressure, knowing that change can happen. I think that it is very important that we know that we are not dreaming, that we are constructing, that we are making a better world and we are going to succeed."* [102]

Carlota Pérez

---

102    The Shaping of a Post-COVID Golden Age, Medium, www.medium.com/presencing-institute-blog/the-shaping-of-a-post-covid-golden-age-de40f75cbb6b

## How can a sustainable organisation have a positive impact on profits?

We mentioned earlier the need for an energy shift and some of the efforts of Banco Brasil, which is no small organisation. They specifically run a programme on energy conservation which promotes the responsible use of electricity at their facilities. For example, in one year their electricity consumption was reduced by 5% compared to 2018.

They run multiple initiatives to reduce electricity consumption. This includes everything from internal awareness-raising activities and acquisition of energy in the free market, to the replacement of fluorescent lamps with LED bulbs and modernisation of air conditioners, which in total translate to avoiding expenses of BRL 14 million. The 27 million kWh saved is enough to supply electricity to more than 12 thousand residences per year.

Being leaner and more sustainable can also be as simple as an effort on toner cartridge refill. For Banco Brasil that translated to BRL 35 million of expenses avoided in 2019 by purchasing reclaimed materials instead of new material from the manufacturer. This switch reduced spend on toner cartridges by over a fifth as well as keeping over 85 thousand used toner cartridges out of landfill.

If you have the infrastructure, start investing in solar panels for your buildings. Solar power helps small and medium sized businesses improve profitability without changing their business model. For example Ørsted integrated a 40MW storage facility into the design of its Permian Energy Center.

Energy savings are straightforward to forecast as panel efficiency and average sunlight are known and predictable. For any standard-sized business, an energy efficiency performance in simple terms could look like this over time:

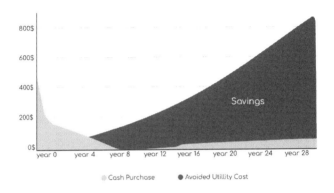

*Figure 3.1: Cash purchases versus avoided utility cost graph, where savings benefits from compound overtime.*

Figure 3.1 is a graph showing the cost of energy on the Y-Axis ranging from USD 0 to USD 800,00, and the number of years on the X-Axis, ranging from 0 to 29. The cash purchases of energy fall steeply from just over USD 400,000 to less than USD 200,000 in the first year, then less steeply to almost 0 by year 8, followed by a very gradual rise to less than USD 50,000 by year 29. This contrasts sharply with the avoided utility costs which rise steadily from 0 at the beginning to USD 800,000 by year 29.

In slightly more comprehensive terms, you can take advantage of the International Performance Measurement and Verification Protocol to measure your energy efficiency:

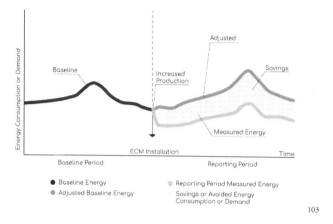

*Figure 3.2: IPMVP graph, includes baseline and reporting period on energy consumption. Adapted from www.evo-world.org*

The graph in Figure 3.2 shows energy consumption or demand on the Y-Axis and the Baseline Period followed by the Reporting Period on the X-Axis. The line showing energy consumption in the baseline period is fairly flat with a rise and fall in the middle. The reporting period compares predicted energy consumption based on increased production against reported consumption following an ECM Installation. The predicted line follows the same pattern as the baseline period, but is higher to reflect more production. This is compared with the reported energy consumption which initially falls sharply

---

103      *International Performance Measurement and Verification Protocol (IPMVP)*, EVO, https://evo-world.org/en/products-ser-vices-mainmenu-en/protocols/ipmvp

followed by a similar consumption pattern, but at a lower level, showing a clear energy saving across the period.

We have this tendency to think about acquiring to support acceleration. Yet, by making the most of what we do have, we become leaner and increase profit.

As an overall summary of Banco do Brasil, their total loan portfolio has grown 9% from 4Q/2019 to 4Q/2020, achieving BRL 742 billion. Over the same period, the sustainable portfolio on average has made up 32%, and has shown a higher growth rate than the total portfolio, accounting for a 12% increase ending up at BRL 244.7 billion. Moreover, in 1Q/2021 the sustainable portfolio was BRL 261.3, or 34% of the total loan portfolio. The sustainability efforts implemented during 2020 played a key role last year, resulting in a annual market ROE of 12.1% at the end of 2020.[104]

**Eating disruption for breakfast**

Think of the zero marginal cost phenomena.[105] Digitisation has brought significant opportunities, which we can adopt and use to experiment with new business models, ideas and ways of working. It can't be zero actual cost, as we need to be relentlessly experimenting with new business ideas and improving technical capabilities. Instead of just concentrating on what you are already doing to be more efficient, your aim is

104     *Results Center,* Banco Do Brasil, https://ri.bb.com.br/en/financial-information/results-center/

105     Big Think, *Jeremy Rifkin on the Fall of Capitalism and the Internet of Things,* YouTube, www.youtube.com/watch?v=3x-OK2aJ-0Js

impact; making changes which pay for themselves, hence your marginal costs of zero. It's about making your efforts effective.

> *"In a digitally connected society, the marginal costs of an increasing number of goods and services would fall to near zero. This would force a fundamental change in prevailing business models: from markets to networks, from ownership to access, from workers to 'prosumers', from sellers and buyers to providers and users, and from consumerism to sustainability — and the second industrial revolution's economies of scale would no longer apply."*[106]

> Jeremy Rifkin

With the digitalisation of products and services, new business models have emerged, from on-demand to subscription and also platform as services.[107] A 2017 McKinsey Digital Global Survey found only 8% of organisations believed their business models would remain economically viable in a digital economy.[108]

Digitising services can enable truly fractal organisations, with a focus on the connective structures over individual components. Which—if done well and flexibly enough—can enable near zero marginal costs at scale. Where you act as the connector. An increase in consumption does not necessarily equal increase in infrastructure, maintenance and support; nor the extraction of

---

106    Big Think, *Jeremy Rifkin on the Fall of Capitalism and the Internet of Things,* YouTube, www.youtube.com/watch?v=3x-OK2aJ-0Js

107    *Platform As A Service,* Wikipedia, www.en.wikipedia.org/wiki/Platform_as_a_service

108    Jacques Bughin, Tanguy Catlin, Martin Hirt and Paul Willmott, *Why digital strategies fail,* McKinsey Digital, www.mckinsey.com/business-functions/mckinsey-digital/our-insights/why-digital-strategies-fail

use of materials and the energy consumption it needs to sustain the increase. For example a bank which digitises statements can not only maintain the same infrastructure, maintenance and support when consumption increases but it is actively decreasing the amount of materials which need to be extracted to support its business and the amount of energy consumed manufacturing and transporting them. Usage and by-products handling is therefore key.

With new technologies, capabilities and computing power, even platforms as services models or professional services require a fundamental investment for relevance and to keep with the cutting edge of what's coming. Otherwise, it's very easy to fall into complacency and become a stale organisation.

Let's also not forget where the digital and physical worlds meet. With the concept of the Internet Of Things, energy, communications and logistics are connected and available at scale. Which role do you play there? How can you be a carbon sink on production and fulfilment? What is the value that your organisation can bring? Not a value to compete but to cooperate and enhance?

> *"Will there soon be a Kondratiev sixth wave of technological change? The one we really need now is a wave of sustainable technologies —ways to produce and mobilize energy and transport ourselves and transport goods, to relieve the massive human pressures and human-caused destruction of the Earth's ecosystems."[109]*
>
> Jeffrey D. Sachs

We find the practice of business acquisition and mergers to support growth, on the side of what can be a negative disruption. Whether acquiring and merging companies or not

---

109     Jeffrey D. Sachs, *The Age of Sustainable Development* (New York: Columbia University Press, 2015)

may be one of the most important decisions an organisation ever faces. Time and time again, we have seen organisations defeating their purpose by ending up destroying value—rather than acting as acceleration. This instead brings disturbance, confusion and problems all around. The effort becomes all in all costly for time, input and value outcome—with all around stressed and unhappy people.

Let's help ourselves by a paradigm shift from having to being.

# B is for Bet

It's naive to think that one can draw the future with a straight line. We need to set ourselves the ability to inspect and adapt, and do that quickly.

Having upfront detailed plans about the predicted sequence of events in detail when building something in a complex environment is programme suicide. Tuning and adjusting it as we go and learning from it is what wins in our ever-changing world.

> *"Rarely are opportunities presented to you in a perfect way. In a nice little box with a yellow bow on top. 'Here, open it, it's perfect. You'll love it.' Opportunities—the good ones— are messy, confusing and hard to recognize. They're risky. They challenge you."[110]*
>
> Susan Wojcicki

Having small cycles with constant feedback loops enables you to manage the extent of that risk, whilst continuously learning from the challenges—keeping time, budget and quality fixed, while adapting the programme as you go and as you learn.

The value is found in being adaptable, with a deep understanding that new things will emerge and supersede others, it's part

---

110     Johns Hopkins University, *Johns Hopkins University 2014 Commencement Speaker: Susan Wojcicki, YouTube CEO*, YouTube, https://www.youtube.com/watch?v=lPqOdhRW6HE

of nature. That idea of multicellular organisms having the ability to repair and maintain integrity. Reduce waste then; stop draining time, effort and energy trying to define a linear detailed future upfront.

The architecture of our system of flow is to be designed to support fast feedback loops across the organisation. Real feedback from the response of our market. Not from gut feelings, not about who owns the idea nor how much we have already invested in it; but to real consumers' response.

Your system architecture emerges. Because of its own need to adapt to the diverse demand and by the increase in the creative use of it.

For that, you need to have the ability for your flow to work through small cycles, so that you can go to market earlier, get a constant flow of feedback. Get that feedback from the market sooner, start trading earlier, deliver value sooner, learn what works, what doesn't and what's really wanted. You can then inform your next steps with real data rather than guesses.

Resilient, profitable organisations don't put all their eggs in one basket.

Start your business ideas as a bet, a small something, so that you can feed it through your flow. And a bet with defined measures that changes on a daily basis, so that you can truly monitor and quickly see if the bet is performing as imagined or not. Take bets as experiments not *quick wins*. We are aiming for sustainable profit, not an immediate reward which is deferring expenses until tomorrow.

For *bets* to work, you also need to nurture an environment where it is safe to fail, with experimentation as part of the path. With resilience to overcome setbacks. As we know, things don't always go as expected, and that is to be expected. We need to be pushing the boundaries of knowledge from what proved us wrong, with the courage to reveal flags, admit errors, the humility to test early and adapt rapidly.

Additionally, make decisions based on the sustainability of the efforts. Quick wins are overrated and can easily damage long term ability to endure. From stock price drop, to job losses and no longer viable businesses; these are potential outcomes of decisions based on narrow-minded and selfish decisions.

The visibility and scrutiny of those decisions is as high as it's ever been, impact on those and economies and livelihoods are at stake. Therefore the gears are turning. There are investors out there that are informed and increasingly more interested. Investors that are, in fact, making their trading decisions based on long-term factors of conscious choices, and that is where the trade is gearing to[111]. Interest from the board of directors to financial investors is becoming more inquisitive: Are you investing in your workers? Promoting diversity? Reducing climate change?

**Constant diagnosis loop**

We touched on the scientific method, from hypothesis to experiments, so that we can learn, so that we can be proven wrong. Find that out earlier on, so that we can reduce waste.

You may have come across the concept of *shifting left* from software testing. Shifting left is the idea of incorporating feedback and testing really early and throughout the development cycle. It supports and integrates assurance, confidence and trust in the product as it's being enhanced. Automatically and continuously. Superpowered by the incorporation of being notified right away if something is not behaving as expected; bringing the concept of monitoring not just for usage but for performance.

---

111      *Sustainable Signals: Individual Investor Interest Driven by Conviction, Impact and Choice*, Morgan Stanley
www.morganstanley.com/content/dam/msdotcom/infographics/
sustainable-investing/Sustainable_Signals_Individual_Investor_
White_Paper_Final.pdf

There is a balance and a connotation to be surfaced here. Fast feedback loops on experiment outcomes and embedding shifting left on quality, are based on factual use. Use from real customers to real plumbing. With plumbing I mean the confidence in the connections and performance of the system to deliver the supply of your product and services.

What may be stopping you placing bets on factual use? We hear often about *scope creep*, yet you can observe in organisations today *bureaucracy creep*. That's a dangerous one.

Bureaucracy creep is the act of slowly and steadily increasing an excessively complicated administrative procedure, which happens unnoticed. Can take many forms like little process changes, extra steps, policy updates… This slows you down.

One of the areas that is heavily hit by bureaucracy creep is the so-called discovery process. Which, in traditional linear approaches, is the process of collecting and analysing information about the project beforehand. When we do know that in fact, the beginning of a project is when you know the least that you are ever going to know about it. Instead, shift from discovery to diagnosis.

Diagnosis of your bets. All ideas are ultimately bets, which are defined as risking something, usually a sum of money, against someone else's on the basis of the outcome of a future event, such as the result of a race or game. We can then describe a business idea as a risk of value—time, effort, intelligence and money—against other competitors', on the basis of the outcome of an unpredictable market and an ever-changing environment.

And bets, ideas, tries, experiments… When these flourish, it makes a difference, opens possibilities, crafts new paths— some which you may not have thought of before. It's what keeps the organisation afloat, what gives you an advantage over other brands and what, ultimately, brings the return on investment. Enabling your system to build its own version of neuroplasticity.[112]

But don't risk it all and don't risk it blindly. Just as Tim Ferriss nicely puts it, because something has been a lot of work or consumed a lot of time doesn't necessarily make it productive or worthwhile.[113]

Focus on the identification of the nature of a problem by examination of the symptoms. Craft hypotheses in line with those symptoms, generate statements per each and outline minuscule bets that can shed some light on how products are actually used to decide if to pivot or persevere.

> *"And then comes the ultimate test: What did the customer do differently as a result?"[114]*
>
> Karen Mangia

It's similar to what Geoff Moore named *crossing the chasm*. Many of the bets will fail to make it from one side to another "of the chasm"—early adopters to early majority. To be able to make the jump and survive it, the product has to solve a real ongoing need for a lot of people, most products aren't compelling enough to cross this chasm and spread.

**How you organise yourself matters**

To be able to feed those small bets of business ideas and capture real feedback, your system map needs to be able to

---

112    The ability of the brain to form and reorganise synaptic connections, especially in response to learning or experience or following injury.

113    Tim Ferriss, *Killing Your Job,* Fast Company, www.fastcompany.com/1718578/killing-your-job

114    Karen Mangia, *Listen Up!: How to Tune In to Customers and Turn Down the Noise* (Hoboken: Wiley, 2021)

support that. Crafted within self-sustained, rapid and dynamic entities that can perform such bets and collect the fluctuating daily metrics.

Just like software system architecture, which is called *soft* for a reason.

For example, Unilever has a clear understanding that to be an industry-leading business they need to move in faster and smarter ways across all levels of their company. That means evolving their culture to encourage more flexibility, agility and accountability.

They launched Flex Experiences, a *space* via a platform, which offers employees the chance to share their talent and experience with people on other teams and in other countries. They are already live in 20 business areas, and so far it has reached over 40 thousand people in more than 100 countries and unlocked over 100 thousand hours of new career experiences and learning. To support this, and the goals of flexibility, agility and accountability, they also adapted what management actually means: to encourage employees to set goals throughout the year with a focus on more innovative, entrepreneurial ways of working.

These efforts started back in 2019 as a pilot with 30 agile teams. So far, Unilever has found that the results have been positive hence its current expansion to other teams.

Flex Experiences has encompassed a range of opportunities, from online extensive training on skilling up and enabling everyone to find their core, to working with the European Works Council on a Framework for the Future of Work. This last one as a specific example includes support for setting up small businesses, to ensure the people affected by automation in their tea plantations in Kericho, Kenya could successfully move from job to job.

One of the key learnings for Unilever from those efforts is that to become a more agile organisation, they need to simplify and flatten the internal structures, and to work in a more networked way. Remember fractal organisations or networking capabilities? Encouraging people to make smarter decisions faster, and with customers and consumers front of mind. With a clear focus: to be a diverse and inclusive workplace where people with purpose thrive.

Profitwise, in the 2020 annual report Unilever showcased its results according to the business cycle 2017-2020.[115] In particular, Unilever has defined the Sustainability Progress Index—included in the Management co-investment plan for managers—a settled target that should fall in between 0% and 200%. The value achieved at the end of 2020 was 124%. Out of all performance metrics, that index was the fuel for positive results in the Return of Invested Capital, a 18% growth in 2020 compared to 2017. Part of these sustainable efforts were driven by a 50% reduction of $CO_2$ emissions compared with 2018 results, including a push up of 20% in sustainable sourced agricultural raw materials. Despite the challenging 2020 year for supply chains, due to COVID-19, that meant a 6.3% decrease in its Return on Invested Capital (ROIC) for this company—yet showed a 15% increase in its Return on Assets (ROA).

Adaptation and change are innate. We need to become *bet ready*.

It's very important that the measures you define for your bets to be tested in the market are some which change often, at least on a daily basis if not more. So that you can shiftly tune up further bets and reduce waste. You don't want to be waiting a fortnight or a month to find out that a bet was pushing items in the wrong direction.

---

115    *Purpose-led, future-fit. Unilever Annual Report and Accounts 2020*, Unilever, www.unilever.com/Images/annual-report-and-accounts-2020_tcm244-559824_en.pdf

## How can your feedback loops radiate rounds of diagnosis?

Information radiator is a term I use often. It encapsulates the idea of availability of data which is highly visible at a glance.

For the different programmes we have spoken about so far, the artefacts that you are co-creating and the hypothesis with the best results—all of that is just so much goodness to have locked down or buried away.

Those things depict your system map and generate insight, that is to guide your steps. Make it available.

An information radiator available on-demand. With on-demand, I mean on pull action rather than push. When we are close to something we want to communicate and tend to push things downstream. We do so because we care about it, we have invested time and effort and because we believe it's important so we distribute it out.

Now, from the receiver's perspective they are also investing time and effort, focus and care towards common goals; they have information being distributed towards them from all angles and channels. Information overload is a serious issue, there is so much and so varied and from so many channels, types and forms; we just can't consume it all.

It's important to carefully consider how to collect it, structure it, and where it lives so that it can be handled. As a side note example from Unilever, they use tools to fetch ideas from the whole organisation, with more than 47 thousand employees from 80 countries contributing over 2 thousand ideas. Over 17 thousand people then voted for their favourites, some of which are already underway. Don't neglect your best jewel: the individuals that bring your organisation alive. An essential driving force, which is closer to the products and services, to the customers and communities you serve; they very well can identify areas and opportunities within your operating system to be better.

So, how can your artefacts and related information radiate so that it can be consumed for value? It must be in a highly visible location, yes a virtual one works. It must be within context, easy to digest and examine. Where could common landing places be for it? What options are there to display that are highly visible and accessible for all? Experiment with it!

The concept of bets partially mimics the process of natural selection. Or how Eric D. Beinhocker extrapolates the idea of Diversify-Select-Amplify to economy and society with the concept of performing small scale policy experiments, test out interventions, do so with variety, and with observation so that we can put a stop to the ones that don't work and scale up those that do.[116] How can this work in your organisation?

Ultimately the biggest insights are going to be driven by experimentation.

### Are the products that you are selling really benefiting customers?

Product ethics is a thing, and an underlying theme throughout this book. An ethical product is often described as an offering that does not cause any harm, either to its users or the planet. We can do better than that. We need to flip that meaning in two ways: one, an ethical product benefits customers (rather than avoiding harm) and; two, we should pursue product ethics by design.

With the embodied transparency that you are acquiring with your system map, practices and information radiators; be careful what you measure. For example, just because we can measure clicks from a notification in our app, does not mean we should target, increase, extend it. Doing so has repercussions not only on the efforts and focus within your organisation but also has

---

116     Eric D. Beinhocker, *The Origin Of Wealth: Evolution, Complexity, and the Radical Remaking of Economics* (London: Random House Business, 2007)

a direct effect on your consumers' well-being—dopamine, anxiety and repercussions on reward pathways.[117]

After all, what matters is how good the product is, the value it brings and how available it is. If you are going to measure something, measure what helps to bring that value sooner in a safer and happier way.[118]

For example, 2.5 billion people use Unilever products every day, they have consumers in over 190 countries and their products are available in 25 million retail sales outlets. Through its Consumer Carelines, Unilever had over 3 million interactions through calls, emails, letters, social media and web chats. That is no small operation. Yet they have:

- Reduced the water used in manufacturing by 47% per tonne of production since 2008

- Achieved a 65% reduction in $CO_2$ from energy per tonne of production since the same year

- Reduced the waste impact per consumer use by 32% since 2010

- Achieved a 96% reduction in total waste per tonne of production since 2008

- Increased by 62% the proportion of raw agricultural materials which were sustainably sourced in 2019

And it's not just at operational level; their leadership engages with NGOs and policymakers to drive system change, the Chief Supply Chain Officer is part of the World Economic Forum (WEF) community focused on supply chains, the CEO works with the Ellen MacArthur Foundation and with WEF on driving the circular economy, among other things.

---

117    Trevor Haynes, *Dopamine, Smartphones & You: A battle for your time,* SITN, https://sitn.hms.harvard.edu/flash/2018/dopamine-smartphones-battle-time

118    IT Revolution, *Better Value Sooner Safer Happier - Jon Smart,* YouTube, www.youtube.com/watch?v=ZKrhdyjGoM8

As well as sustainability progress, this all produces measurable profit. By reducing energy from its factories by 29% per tonne of production from 2008 to 2019, Unilever saved around EUR 733 million.

Are your products and services really benefiting society? As you fine-tune on this journey to become sustainable, happy and profitable, you must play an active interest in the ripples that our adjustments and decisions are having. Just like the Future of Work program from Unilever ensuring that people affected could easily, happily and sustainably be redeployed. How does this idea translate to your context? What's your primary measure?

# C is for Connect

With an accelerated rhythm and constant flow of bets through your system, you need to take it up a notch and *connect the dots.*

In a study by a coalition of organisations working with influential businesses and investors, it was estimated that companies experience an average internal rate of return of 27% to 80% on their low carbon investments.[119] These businesses recognise that the transition to a low carbon economy is the only way to secure sustainable economic growth and prosperity for all—with the focus of amplifying the business voice, pragmatic climate action by all and advancing smart policy frameworks.

Having the awareness of organisations being operating systems, you can then look beyond the mechanism of an organisation to the organism. This can be done through better management of natural resources like water and energy, as well as minimising waste and improving well-being.

Individuals—CEOs, CFOs, CTOs, VPs, Heads of Department, Team Leads, you name it—we have what it takes to do so.

- Visualise things,
- Deliver often,

---

119     *The Climate Has Changed: Why bold, low carbon action makes good business sense.,* We Mean Business, https://s3.amazonaws.com/assets.wemeanbusinesscoalition.org/wp-content/uploads/2014/09/03183839/The-Climate-Has-Changed_3.pdf

- Involve real users,
- Automate repeatable things,
- Uniqueness of people,
- Specialised skills,
- Processes that work for you,
- Network effects,
- Experiment and learn constantly,
- Higher pace of innovation,
- Enjoy the ride,
- Be a force for good.

Warren Buffet popularised the term *moat*, highlighting how castles were encircled by moats—deep ditches of water—for protection and explains that organisations should create similar shields from competition. The above list is my take on how modern organisations can gain a competitive edge-not by taking away from others but making the most. How today organisations can thrive and make a difference in their time; rather than legacy things like protected intellectual property, years of brand building, substantial control of a distribution channel etc.

Missing out by not *connecting the dots,* affects us in a similar manner to the negative effects of acquisition disruption. When a strategy is used for the wrong reasons and where conflict of interest takes over, we fail our organisation, our team and ourselves. Missing out by not connecting happens also when slipping into complacency, when there is lack of Research and Development. How do we solve this? One can fix these behaviours by having a large amount of skin in the game, by infusing diversity of thinking. That also includes the board and investors, as in today's economies they have a larger role to play, to not only benefit their individual interests but mostly society.

> *"Whatever anybody says or does, assume positive intent. You will be amazed at how your whole approach to a person or problem becomes very different."[120]*

Indra Nooyi

Connecting the dots is a combination of factors rather than innovation by osmosis. You can observe this intent to innovate by osmosis quite clearly through the common belief that innovation can be achieved by buying technology. The expectations are often too high of either a specific technology capability or an external technology 'god' to save you from all your troubles. It just doesn't work that way. Technology can certainly be an enabler, but doesn't do much by itself.

To effectively connect the dots we must seek social cohesion, which is based on mutual respect and the ability to help others. Integrated thinking by active consideration of the relationship, components, gaps and outcomes. Connecting the dots is the art of enhancing the image created. When connecting the dots, something is revealed.

### The distraction landscape

Too much information, too much choice, too much noise and too many ideas. We have been living in the age of distraction.

A few years ago, I came across this Marketing Technology Landscape Supergraphic. Since 2011, they have been collecting the options within the MarTech options landscape. And yes, you guessed it, it has been exponentially growing year on year. One in five of the solutions on the 2020 MarTech landscape weren't there the previous year.

---

120     Indra Nooyi, *The best advice I ever got,* Fortune, https://archive.fortune.com/galleries/2008/fortune/0804/gallery.bestadvice.fortune/7.html

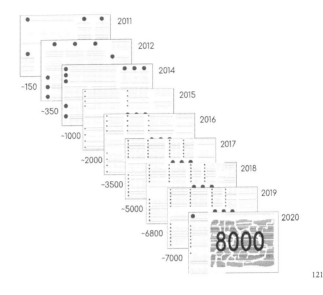

*Figure 3.3: Marketing Technology Landscape Supergraphic, exponential increment of systems available options from 2011 to 2020. Adapted from Chiefmartec.*

That is from 2011 when they started collecting this data; you can see how it has and it is still growing. Figure 3.3 represents maps of marketing technology available options each year from 2011 to 2020. The approximate number of systems solutions each year is 150, 350, 1000, 2000, 3500, 5000, 6800, 7000 and 8000. It's not slowing down. And that is just the marketing technology arena. Imagine the current picture of the full stack technology landscape. With this sea of endless options, how easy is it to get distracted?

121     Scott Brinker, *Marketing Technology Landscape Super-graphic (2020): Martech 5000 — really 8,000, but who's counting?*, chiefmartec, www.chiefmartec.com/2020/04/marketing-technology-landscape-2020-martech-5000

We put way too much effort into influencing and purchasing technology. With so many ideas (which is a healthy thing), way too much choice and so much noise it can easily drain efforts, bring confusion and polarised goals.

Start with the problem, is what we are often told. Yet, 'the' problem may not be known, so with the best intentions we end up chucking time, effort, technology and funds to other things. We need to be learning where to aim for the best return on efforts.

Hence the importance of systems thinking, of your visual representation of your system map. So that you can break free of that spiral of self-destruction. Having that depiction of how your value flows through the system brings to the surface bottlenecks that need to be addressed.

Remember the idea to *test before you invest*? Tests are part of the system, and they are part of its architecture just like any other part of the system is. How are your bets and test funneling through the system map? They are to support development so it should not impact operations, and that's how it should be designed.

Having a common direction and the aim to constantly reduce waste is a collaborative effort. To work on the areas that are slowing the system down requires flexibility and the understanding throughout the fractal organisation that there is one horizon. Via maximising the utilisation of bets as a starting point to kill the often found pre-conception of 'them and us'. In an organisation—from individual, team, department, supplier, partner, etc.—you have just one vision.

The entity of 'them' may often take the form of 'The Business', as if there is an imagined body higher up the ladder of bureaucracy. It's just an imaginary entity. You are not trapped in a system.

You can choose your own systems! In software architecture you commonly find the so-called Dependency Rule pattern.[122] It is a system which is structured in layers, like an onion where source code dependencies point inwards. The CEO is at the centre (as opposed to the top) so is in a supporting and enabling position, a servant leader. Unlike a ladder, which topples if a rung breaks, a problem in a layer of an onion can be mitigated by the others. Overcoming the bottlenecks is therefore a collective effort, with everyone trying to fine-tune and become more effective as they go. Think about communication as allowing easy access to expert users—network capabilities—therefore fading the lines between 'them and us'.

Details from the outer layers shouldn't matter, for example in software a particular interface or device should be easily dropped when it no longer serves a useful purpose. Remember autotomy? Being regenerative by design—people, planet and profit.

### Staying still is actually going backwards

Connecting the dots is a journey to see the bigger picture and to pursue better, not a destination. The components are interdependent but also sound entities in their own right, all trying to do what they do best to support others to flourish as an integral part of the whole.

Although it may seem a big kick start effort to become sustainable, happy and profitable—it can be gradual. And

---

122     Robert C. Martin (Uncle Bob), *The Clean Architecture,* The Clean Code Blog, https://blog.cleancoder.com/uncle-bob/2012/08/13/the-clean-architecture.html#:~:text=t=The%20Dependency%20Rule&text=In%20general%2C%20the%20further%20in,dependencies%20can%20only%20point%20inwards

once progress is in motion you get the benefits of momentum, gearing it towards good impact.

In 2008, Neal's Yard Remedies looked holistically at their emissions across the company's operations, including its premises and business travel. Since then, they have been a CarbonNeutral® company. This effort is also supporting its core, the brand's focus on promoting ethical and environmentally-friendly products to customers in the US, the UK and around the world.

They are an example of a high street brand that has sustained and thrived over the years, their mission is to "enhance and protect people's health and well-being, which starts with the very first seed long before the ingredients arrive to their eco factory", and it pays off. According to their 2019 financial report, Neal's Yard Remedies (home) Ltd has GBP 6 million in total assets, a working capital of GBP 4 million and net profit of GPB 635 thousand.[123] Not bad.

For internal reductions, the company set a Science Based Target for a 47% reduction in emissions intensity by 2025 and an 87% reduction by 2050.[124] To date, the company has cut its emission intensity by 19%. The Science Based Target in simple terms is the commitment to reduce carbon emissions to tackle climate change, it's science-based when it runs in line with the scale of reductions required to keep global temperature increase below 2°C above pre-industrial temperatures.

---

123    *Neal's Yard Remedies (Home) Limited,* Global Database,    www.uk.globaldatabase.com/company/neal-s-yard-remedies-home-limited

124    *Sustainable ingredients ethically sourced,* Neal's Yard Remedies,    www.nealsyardremedies.com/about-us-pages/beliefs/sustainability.html

Neal's Yard Remedies has used the emissions data captured for its CarbonNeutral® certification to set robust targets for year on year emissions reductions in different areas. It has delivered this in part through renewable electricity installation and procurement, for example they have 700m² of solar panels at its eco-factory in Dorset, which generates more than 5% of its electricity. It tops this up with 100% UK-sourced renewable electricity and by choosing 100% renewable electricity and gas for its retail stores.

Its packaging is Carbon Balanced through the World Land Trust™, which means that they offset the amount of $CO_2$ used to make their packaging by protecting tropical forest. Since 2012 they've helped save over 1,000,000m² of endangered forest, offsetting 250 tonnes of $CO_2$.

The company's carbon neutral goal has also been met by financing emission reduction projects that build low carbon sustainable development, such as the Makira Forest Protection Project in Madagascar.[125] The Makira project plays an essential role in biodiversity protection by limiting deforestation in the Makira Natural Park—a protected area of 372 thousand hectares—and works with communities around the forest in a 'protection zone' of 350 thousand hectares to develop sustainable livelihoods. The main quantitative goal is delivering approximately 1.2 million tonnes of emission reductions each year.

By starting these efforts, achieving certification and focussing on their core, they have supported the brand and returns as

---

125    *Makira REDD+, Madagascar: Conserving important biodiversity by empowering 50,000 community members to build sustainable livelihoods,* Natural Capital Partners, www.naturalcapitalpartners.com/projects/project/madagascar-makira-redd#

well as extending that support outwards into communities. And it doesn't stop there.

Neal's Yard Remedies work closely with their suppliers and have built strong, lasting relationships with growers who use organic, fair trade and wild-harvesting practices. In 2017, they paid more than GBP 30 thousand in fair trade premiums to suppliers to support local communities and funded projects including building a well for the women of the Samburu Tribe, who collect their Kenyan frankincense.[126]

Neal's Yard Remedies have the world's largest collection of Soil Association certified health and beauty products, with 64% of their relevant formulations currently certified organic, and 100% of their cotton. They intend to certify their non-organic products under the new COSMOS Natural standard by 2025.

It's a continuous improvement effort for years, it pays off.

### Quick wins and quick losses

As a result of the latest report of the Intergovernmental Panel on Climate Change (IPCC), some countries are marching to the goal of carbon neutrality by 2050, more explicitly included in the global agreement being negotiated for adoption in Paris in 2015. The argument is that to avoid exceeding a 2 degree celsius rise, we have to set out the trajectory for achieving zero global emissions by 2050.

---

126     *Frankincense* is an aromatic gum resin obtained from an African tree which is then used as incense.

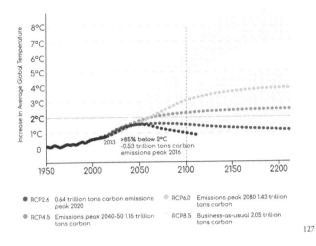

127

*Figure 3.4: Global Temperature Projections for various Representative Concentration Pathways scenarios. Emissions peak and cumulative carbon budgets are for fossil fuel $CO_2$-only emissions. Adapted from IPCC.*

Figure 3.4 is a graph showing the increase in average global temperature on the Y-Axis and the years from 1950 to 2200 on the X-Axis. The trajectory shows that by 2100, if we continue with business as usual the increase in average global temperature is likely to be above 5 degrees celsius. With pathway 6.0 and pathway 4.5, the increase is expected to be 3 degrees celsius and just above 2 degrees celsius respectively. The Representative Concentration Pathways 2.6 keeps the trajectory just below 2 degrees celsius. Looking at the related data and trajectory, I personally think that we should be aiming to keep it under 1.5 degrees celsius and also shifting dates to reach carbon neutrality by 2030. It's certainly not an easy challenge but we

---

127    *Introducing the roadmap to zero emissions,* Architecture 2030.org,    www.architecture2030.org/introducing-the-road-map-to-zero-emissions

need to remember that not all of the repercussions of emissions that we have already made are yet perceived in temperature rise in the atmosphere.

There are two main ways we can theoretically achieve carbon neutrality by 2050. One is based on 100% per cent renewable energy—utilising energy efficiency at scale to reduce energy demand, and simultaneously decentralising and decarbonising power generation and transmission so renewables can make a stable contribution.

The second way is with a high share of renewables but using technologies that result in 'negative emissions'. A concept has emerged recently to describe the possible use of bio-energy with carbon capture and storage (BECCS) to produce negative $CO_2$ emissions by combining biomass use with geologic carbon capture and storage (CCS). To simplify, as we know that crops absorb $CO_2$ as they grow, this BECCS concept is to leverage that natural system using the crops which are then burned in a power station; the resulting $CO_2$ from this processing is captured and then buried in wells, mines or geologic formations underground or under the sea. Electricity generation using BECCS then theoretically becomes a net absorber of $CO_2$ rather than a net emitter. In theory, achieving carbon neutrality could be easier if CCS and BECCS could be scaled up cost-effectively. Yet in real life there are very few projects that show this to be the case.[128] Think of the enormous amount of land and water needed to grow the crops that then are to be burned; this process could also worsen food and water security, especially for the world's poor—adding to climate injustice. BECCS is not a feasible solution. In fact, it can have big detrimental consequences. As Adam Vaughan, the chief reporter at New Scientist magazine, puts it, "The technology,

---

128     David Schlissel and Dennis Wamsted, *IEEFA U.S.: Ratepayers face risks with Project Tundra's retrofit of aging N.D. coal-fired plant,* IEEFA, www.ieefa.org/ieefa-u-s-ratepayers-face-risks-with-project-tundras-retrofit-of-aging-n-d-coal-fired-plant

known as bioenergy with carbon capture and storage (BECCS), could prove a cure worse than the disease, at least when it comes to water stress."[129] We are left with the ugly truth that we need to deal with the problem head on—no weird patches and workarounds.

As you navigate towards carbon neutrality, a better bet is becoming a carbon sink—resulting in 'negative emissions'. For this, you will need to balance emissions with absorptions. As a temporary measure you could be offsetting a surplus of emissions, how can it work in the long run?

A carbon credit, often called carbon offset, is a credit for greenhouse emissions reduced or removed from the atmosphere from an emission reduction project, which can be used by governments, industry or private individuals to compensate for the emissions they are generating.

Carbon credits are typically measured in tonnes of $CO_2$-equivalents and are bought and sold through a number of international brokers, online retailers and trading platforms. Businesses can purchase carbon credits to offset their emissions by making finance readily available to renewable energy projects, forest protection, and reforestation projects around the world.

Offsetting one tonne of carbon means there will be one less tonne of $CO_2$ in the atmosphere than there would otherwise have been. For example, when solar energy companies sell carbon offsets, this helps them as these projects become more viable. The buyers of the offsets benefit as they can use these offsets to mitigate their GHG emissions. Carbon offsets enable countries to scale green projects, change the energy mix more readily and contemplate more environmentally sound policies.

---

129  Adam Vaughan, *Carbon negative crops may mean water shortages for 4.5 billion people,* New Scientist, www.newscientist.com/article/2270227-carbon-negative-crops-may-mean-water-shortages-for-4-5-billion-people

Don't be naive with carbon offsets. This is not a sustainable solution and I don't advocate much for it. We must treat the source of the problem, a clear up later approach doesn't work. It's like consciously growing your technical debt, the more time elapses from fixing the problem the more difficult and expensive it becomes.

Have a good look at your visual circular economy and flow of operations—scrutinising it is a good thing. What are we doing *xyz* for? If we were to solve this problem for the first time how would we solve it? The ability to really question the *why* of doing something, the purpose of things you have in place today, is a tool to readjust the <u>focus</u> on what matters and to free up time to <u>do</u> what really matters. Also a constant scrutiny on a search for a better way to solve something with small adjustments helps you to elevate to new highs.

This is a mindset which can spread across the organisation, through your whole value chain, along the communities that you touch and then on via their influence. Beyond what a single product or service reach could ever do.

# Call. Be. Act.

*"Today we have economies that need to grow, whether or not they make us thrive: what we need are economies that make us thrive, whether or not they grow."*[130]

Kate Raworth

### Measure the return on sustainable investment

Make up your own framework, just as Elopak has done. *Copycat* strategies just don't work. Frameworks don't have your interests at heart, they can't, as they don't know your organisation. Context is everything.

One of course can enrich the efforts by being inspired, for example the ROSI methodology is good at providing tools to measure the Return on Sustainable Investment.[131] This is the underlying theme we have been covering, of embedding sustainability into core business strategy, decision-making, and

---

130     Kate Raworth, *Doughnut Economics: Seven Ways to Think Like a 21st-Century Economist* (New York: Random House, 2018)

131     *Center for Sustainable Business | Return on Sustainability Investment (ROSI™)*, NYU Stern, www.stern.nyu.edu/experience-stern/about/departments-centers-initiatives/centers-of-research/center-sustainable-business/research/return-sustainability-investment-rosi

accounting and quantifying the range of costs and benefits (social, environmental and yes financial).

## Become carbon neutral certified

Work to attain a carbon neutral certification and reduce energy consumption whilst avoiding costs, then officially seek a carbon neutral recognised certification by applying for a global validated entity at www.carbonneutral.com which uses science-based targets as mentioned.

## Compensate for emissions

Even though you cannot reduce emissions to zero on day 1, you can compensate for the emissions by supporting emission reduction programs outside of your value chain until at least you get there.

For example, Elopak offset all its company emissions in addition to emissions related to carbon neutral packages delivered to its customers. Since 2016 Elopak has compensated for approximately 248 thousand tonnes $CO_2$e. To do that, some Elopak units are still reporting business travel in an internal reporting system.

Business travel is an example where you can make a big impact on the reduction of emissions whilst balancing a bare minimum with carbon credits, while you demonstrate investments and best practices to reduce your GHG emissions. There are lots of organisations that help business to buy carbon credits, for example:

- www.goldstandard.org (Gold Standard is the standard used to verify projects)
- www.secondnature.org/climate-action-guidance/purchasing-carbon-offsets-faqs
- www.green-e.org/certified-resources/carbon-offsets
- www.carboncreditcapital.com/carbon-credits

- www.onecarbonworld.com/shop
- www.carbonfund.org
- www.cooleffect.org
- www.terrapass.com

**Check where you invest**

It's important to note that carbon offsets are not regulated at this point, you have to make sure that your intermediary is from a reputable source and controlled by internationally recognised third parties. You should look for a mention of the Gold Standard strict vetting system or the Verified Carbon Standard (VCS), which is a global benchmark standard for project-based, voluntary, GHG emission reductions and removals. VCS was developed by The Climate Group, the International Emissions Trading Association (IETA), the World Business Council for Sustainable Development (WBCSD) and a range of business, government and non-government organizations. So that you can ensure that your carbon offsets have oversight from a trustworthy third party.

**Network for greening the financial system**

In addition to the WBCSD, central banks across the globe have created the Network for Greening the Financial System. Its purpose is that businesses can better report on how their activities have an impact on the environment, which in turn enables central banks to better design incentives that enable companies to switch to cleaner models of production, support economic activity and address climate risk.

**Make an impact locally**

Be there to serve your customers, to serve society. Get involved with local and global funds that support health, education, safer water and sanitation, small holder and responsible farming, access for all to low-carbon energy resources and mechanisms to protect biodiversity.

One of the social institutions you can tap into is the Sustainable Development Solutions network (www.unsdsn.org/networks-overview), they work closely with businesses and governments around the development and scaling up of new solutions to support the Sustainable Development Goals.

**Aim for zero waste**

Be careful with the distraction landscape and aim for zero waste. Aim for zero waste manufacturing, for example if you are using plastic, check whether other materials, such as glass, may be feasible alternatives. Focus on how you lead on and encourage:

- Recover goods
- Returns and refurb
- Recycle and resale

A materials science approach to eco-design is especially important because 80% of a product's sustainability is pretty much set at the design stage.

Shift to digitise your offerings, from selling services rather than products (printing vs printers).

And zero waste also on efforts:

- Apply the scientific method
- Embed a constant diagnosis loop
- Infuse the effort with information radiators
- How you organise yourself matters

Staying still is actually going backwards.

Sustainably harmonise your growth from material improvement over time with environmental and well-being at heart. This can certainly help the bottom line.

# Last Thoughts

Throughout this book we covered the three flavours of sustainable development: economic development meaning how doing better translates into profit as a result; social inclusion which fosters happiness and superpowers what you do; environmental sustainability with the key role we are to play.

Much of what we covered you already knew. Yet lack of current sustainable happy profit is seen all around; it's borne out of lack of awareness and intention. To be able to cross the chasm and move from cognitive reasoning to making a difference, we must learn by doing. That is also about encompassing ethical thinking which directly impacts the way we behave, develop and the decisions that we take.

The truth is that there isn't a magic wand (an external god or technology) to come and save you, do 'the trick'; otherwise the biggest challenge to the human race to date would have been solved by most and by now.

We must think ahead morally and practically. After all, you are a stakeholder. You have a stake in the product and services that you are involved in building, in the ones you consume and the impact they have in communities, livelihoods and the planet we inhabit—which is not ours alone. Having a *stake* is part of your role, part of your duty and, if you think about it, it's a big part of why you were hired in the first place.

As someone that identifies as a foodie, I tell you that you can't master gastronomy—or for what matters, the concepts of this book—by just reading about it. To get the best from it, you need to get practical and get started.

Take inspiration from the examples, pointers and ideas in this book to identify specific actions you can take today. Being a sustainable, happy and profitable organisation goes beyond checklists and execution of responsibility. It's a deep partnership of the whole, across your value chain, employees, customers and community. More than that, however, it's beyond just who you serve but speaks also about who you are. Change starts within.

The potential that healthy organisations have is beyond doubt. Even for the most sceptical. Global executives that I work with agree with this: focusing on reducing waste from all angles, increase of evaluative happiness and better profits are worth the effort. Lasting. Sustainable. Whole.

The truth is that this superpower is untapped for most entities.

We, humans, are more concerned with <u>having</u> than <u>being</u>, with getting more for less. We can't decouple what we do from what we are.

Being aware is the start. You have HD glasses now at hand, you can choose to wear them or not. When the sociologist Karl Mannheim popularised the idea of *worldview* in late 1920s he explained that, "Every point of view is particular to a social situation". Your point of view can become particular to your new priorities. Your point of view is the lens through which you interpret the world.

We must think sensibly about how people behave in the real world and measure it. Going back to the incentive idea, the so-called nudge policies may have a part to play, yet we can't leave it all to that.[132] Things aren't quite as they seem so we

---

132     "Nudge is a concept in behavioral economics, political theory, and behavioral sciences which proposes positive reinforcement and indirect suggestions as ways to influence the behavior and decision making of groups or individuals." *Nudge theory,* Wikipedia, www.en.wikipedia.org/wiki/Nudge_theory

must measure what matters. Tangible measures that would simultaneously slow climate change, reduce pressure on water, limit nitrogen pollution in the world's waterways and boost human health.

Goals matter. Define the direction, the purpose which will guide our steps. With accountability to follow through and transparency in all the efforts and their progress. Publish it publicly! Accountability, transparency and communicating outcomes are key.

In order to achieve results it's important not to hold back. Acknowledge that you are vulnerable—avoid the *god complex*—so that you can base your organisation on trust. Trust meaning having the confidence that each other's intentions are good and aiming for better highs.

As you work through the measures, rather than traditional forecasting use *backcasting*; the concept of defining the desirable future and working backwards for it to happen. This change of lens sets the tone for a common understanding of variation and adjustment as part of the process, with the sole focus of the current efforts towards that common goal—that crafted a desirable future. No need to invest time and effort on who and how wrong a forecast was, that's waste. Instead have productive disagreements with the aim to produce the best possible solution in the shortest period of time so you can learn from it. Healthy conflict helps us to reach new highs.

It would be naive to think that you can draw the future with a straight line, we need to embed systems thinking in our efforts towards Sustainable Happy Profit, with constant feedback loops.

And although all entities have baggage, we can't change the past but we can make a conscious dent in crafting the future—a better future. Whichever history your organisation has and the current burdens it may be handling; they are not destiny, they are not fate. They are reasons for action.

We looked at analogies of nature throughout, ecosystems without human disruption are resilient, evolve and thrive for millions of years. There is much to learn from nature design principles, especially about how to organise ourselves. Create an organisation that is regenerative by design, fair and just, where its contributions are greater than the sum of its parts.

Joseph Schumpeter was one of the first authors to develop a theory about evolutionary economics, inspired by biology focussing on the study of processes dealing with complex interdependencies, competition, growth, structural change, and resource constraints.[133]

We learnt how Eric Beinhocker outlines the approach to mimic the process of natural selection of Diversify-Select-Amplify, even for small scale policy experiments to be able test out a range of bets, which you learn from and select the ones that work well to scale up and put a stop to the ones that don't.

> *"Let's face it, the universe is messy. It is nonlinear, turbulent, and chaotic. It is dynamic. It spends its time in transient behaviour on its way to somewhere else, not in mathematically neat equilibria. It self-organises and evolves. It creates diversity, not uniformity. That's what makes the world interesting, that's what makes it beautiful, and that's what makes it work."[134]*

> Donella H. Meadows

Don't get disheartened when things don't work. *Trial and error* are part of the journey. There will be times when we need more trials than others. Experiment with your process to pursue a

---

133     *Evolutionary economics,* Wikipedia, www.en.wikipedia.org/wiki/Evolutionary_economics

134     Donella H. Meadows, *Thinking In Systems: A Primer* (White River Junction: Chelsea Green Publishing, 2008)

happier life. With our days being perishable the least we can do is get the most out of them for a better tomorrow.

An action is better than just talking, so it's ok to commit without having perfect information. Come to terms with uncertainty and change, it's part of nature. Set a system of feedback for all ideas, as part of your system map; find your cause, prioritise well-being, digitise etc. so you have a constant drive with attention to results and their impact.

Evolve your team, department, organisation, community and influence by not just speech and will but by a series of concrete actions on a motion to constantly optimise what you do. It's a journey, not a destination.

An effective system is deployed across a range of tasks at any one time. We must, of course, focus on the whole, but we must learn to also break our focus down to look at the parts. We have a societal culture that is built to distract us from main challenges by creating too much noise and too much choice. Hence the importance of that system perspective, a meta view.

Difficulties arise because we are trying to outline a system whilst we deal with the least linear thing of all, humans. So do it together: set challenges as a problem solving exercise, decide by enriched ideas, try things and run a constant diagnosis loop to inform the next steps. Then repeat.

I hope that through the remarkable stories of the case studies, you can see how companies and institutions are choosing to answer the wake-up call and be an active part of the sustainable solution: implementing responsible practices, goals and ambitious projects.

**Governments** can use policies to either make the carbon-based version of operations and products more expensive, or to make the clean version cheaper. This could include requiring a certain amount of electricity or fuel to be generated in zero-carbon ways (for example, in the UK as part of the diesel banning green hydrogen is part of a policy set).[135]

**Companies** and investors can commit to acquiring and using cleaner alternatives, investing in research and development, supporting clean-energy entrepreneurs and startups and advocating for agile government policies (meaning regulations that allow companies to move fast to take actions like sustainability programs supported by metrics like in our stories).

**Individuals** can help create markets for better with cleaner alternatives by giving strong market signals: when we buy an electric vehicle or a plant-based meal we are taking a stand, and with our choices we drive the making of clean products more affordable and available for everyone.

Understanding the sustainable options that we currently have as well as those we are developing will enable us to work harmoniously with planet Earth to maintain a healthy, balanced world. A regenerative by design macro system.

We need to think honestly about what will happen if we continue with our business as usual. Knowing that the way we do business is not usual, but unusual—highly based in a false sense of security. Then contrast that picture with what we really need to do, which is reshape our own behaviour to create an alternative course of Sustainable, Happy Profit.

Deep down it is really an exercise in problem solving— about being creative tackling economically, socially and environmentally serious concerns. Setting our organisations to be resilient and desirable places to work, missions to contribute to, visions to be part of.

---

135      Nathalie Thomas, David Sheppard and Neil Hume, *The race to scale up green hydrogen,* Financial Times, www.ft.com/content/7eac54ee-f1d1-4ebc-9573-b52f87d00240

We shape the societies we live in—touching hearts and minds in your own business, your community, upstream and downstream on your own supply chain.

You are faced with an opportunity and a choice, to be part of the solution and to how we craft the playing field of organisations.

Take one bit and bite at a time, and you can change the world.

# Acknowledgements

It would be rather lengthy to properly acknowledge all those individuals whose efforts to drive Sustainable, Happy Profit have inspired me. I highly benefited from the vast range of questions and challenges from my colleagues and contracts over the years. Some are mentioned in the book, however many did not find their way into the narrative; by no means are they less important, in many ways are the foundations of this book.

As much interest I had in the subjects at hand, when tackling the challenge set for this book I knew my knowledge was falling short, especially in environmental economics. I had the pleasure to work hand in hand with Dario Martinez, an Argentinian economist with over 14 years' experience in project management roles related to economic policies analysis, their practical implications and impacts assessments. As an economic advisor for bilateral chambers of commerce over the past 7 years, Dario has been responsible for developing market research and multicultural negotiations, supporting small and medium companies. I hope by now you are looking to get involved in initiatives and projects that promote best sustainable practices such as energy efficiency improvements, new technologies for clean energy sources, actionable programs to achieve decarbonisation goals etc. Please have a look at his work linkedIn.com/in/dario-martinez. Thank you Dario for enlightening me and the readers on such important topics. It's been a pleasure working with you at so many levels.

Many people have invested time, care and effort to read and comment on the manuscript in its various stages. Karen Moran your wit and craft once again on editing the early stages of the manuscript, helping me to understand the intricacies and shades of this language. Karen Mangia VP of Customer & Market Insights at Salesforce, thank you for your guiding wise hand in the world of authoring. To Serena Ingre Communications Sustainability & Workforce Innovation at Salesforce, Brendan James Sapato marketer at Ecoalf and Wagner Siqueira member of Brazilian Association of Sustainable Development.

People often ask me how I get to contribute to so many initiatives and how I get to do so many different things. There are multiple factors that enable that to happen, but none of it would be possible without the endless support, patience and love from my wife Helen. This book is no different, yet again she has been a pillar from its inception; my sound board, supportive, encouraging and horizon reminder. Helen, I can't thank you enough for your revisions, corrections, challenges and ideas. Thank you for walking together with me in this journey called life.

# More from Ines

Thank you for reading my book. Now that you've seen what I have to say about building organisations which thrive in their journey of becoming Sustainable, Happy and Profitable; I think it's about time I tell you a bit more about myself.

I grew up in Barcelona where I studied a communications double-degree (five years) with an emphasis on advertising, PR and marketing. I landed in London in 2007 for supposedly a month and, although I call myself a digital-nomad, London has in fact become where I call home.

Over time that communications background brought me to internal communications and business transformation. And whilst digital solutions have an important part to play with evolving a business by acting as an enabler yet by themselves digital solutions don't do very much.

I'm an Agile Coach, a Certified Scrum Professional® (CSP-SM) and a Salesforce MVP. Altogether, I help organisations every day to become more Agile; most often whilst delivering Salesforce technology. I consult, speak and train in these arenas always with the end in mind of empowering a mindset evolution (not revolution). I'm an active member and collaborator on ScrumAlliance.org and AgileAlliance.org.

I'm on a quest to build a sustainable future by enabling customers to have a positive and better impact on well-being, communities and the planet we live in, through all that I do.

If you liked this book you may also like some of my experiments and ideas. Head over to www.getagile.co.uk, where you'll see one of my recent inventions being a game for teams to self-assess, improve and also have a laugh www.theagileretrospectivegame.com

I'd like to stay in touch with you. If you haven't yet, subscribe to my newsletter www.getagile.co.uk/join on my website. You can also follow me on Twitter (@inescapinezka) and on LinkedIn (in/InesGarciaAgile).

If you write a review of this book somewhere I'd love to know what you think, please tag me and add the book hashtag #SustainableHappy.

If you want to share your story through this journey, head over www.SustainableHappyProfit.com. See you on the other side!

# Appendix:
# Carbon Emissions Status

Acommon way to measure carbon emissions is to convert them into $CO_2$ equivalent. A carbon dioxide equivalent ($CO_2$-eq) is a metric measure used to compare the emissions from various GHGs on the basis of their global-warming potential (GWP) by converting amounts of other gases to the equivalent amount of $CO_2$ with the same global warming potential. For example, the GWP for methane is 25 and for nitrous oxide 298. This means that emissions of 1 million metric tonnes of methane and nitrous oxide respectively are equivalent to emissions of 25 and 298 million metric tonnes of $CO_2$.

The GWP describes the relative potency, molecule for molecule, of a GHG, taking account of how long it remains active in the atmosphere. The GWPs currently used are those calculated over 100 years. $CO_2$ is taken as the gas of reference and given a 100-year GWP of 1.

This imbalance between GHG emissions and the ability for natural processes to absorb those emissions has resulted in a continued increase in atmospheric concentrations of GHGs. Concentrations of $CO_2$ in the atmosphere have increased by about 40% since the mid-1800s.

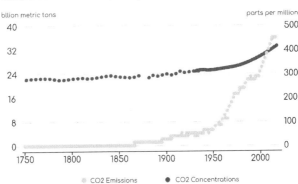

World carbon dioxide (CO2) emissions from fossil fuel combustion and global atmospheric concentrations CO2 (1752-2018)

*Figure A.1: World $CO_2$ emissions from fossil fuel combustion and global atmospheric concentrations from 1752 to 2018. Adapted from www.eia.gov* [136]

Figure A.1 plots $CO_2$ concentrates alongside $CO_2$ emissions from 1750 to 2000. $CO_2$ concentrations rise gradually from 276.4 parts per million (ppm) in 1750 to 311.54 ppm in 1950, after which they increase more rapidly to 405.404 ppm in 2018. The $CO_2$ emissions rise gradually from 0.01 billion metric tons (bmt) in 1750 to 0.54 bmt in 1870, but then increase rapidly to 36.22 billion metric tons in 2018. Around 2007/2008 the $CO_2$ emissions overtook $CO_2$ concentrations.

The World Resources Institute has developed interesting tools to quantify emissions worldwide. The following graphs show historical GHG emissions by regions (www.climatewatchdata.

136     *Energy and the environment explained Greenhouse gases and the climate*, U.S. Energy Information Administration, www.eia.gov/energyexplained/energy-and-the-environment/greenhouse-gases-and-the-climate.php

org/ghg-emissions). Other alternative sites for emissions data reference Global Carbon Project's Carbon Atlas[137] or $CO_2$. earth.[138]

In Figure A.2, the Y-Axis shows $CO_2$e plotted against the X-Axis which shows the years 1990 to 2016. The areas represented on the graph include the World total, East Asia and the Pacific, Europe and Central Asia, the North America region, Latin America and the Caribbean, South Asia, Sub-Saharan Africa, the Middle East and North Africa, and finally the European Union. In 2016 there were 49.36 Gt $CO_2$e, with East Asia and Pacific conjointly with Europe and Central Asia representing around 26 Gt of that annual amount.

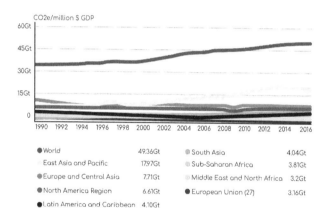

| | | | |
|---|---|---|---|
| ● World | 49.36Gt | ● South Asia | 4.04Gt |
| East Asia and Pacific | 17.97Gt | ● Sub-Saharan Africa | 3.81Gt |
| ● Europe and Central Asia | 7.71Gt | Middle East and North Africa | 3.2Gt |
| ● North America Region | 6.61Gt | ● European Union (27) | 3.16Gt |
| ● Latin America and Caribbean | 4.10Gt | | |

*Figure A.2: World GHG emissions by geographical area from 1990 to 2016.*

---

137    *Global Project's Carbon Atlas,* Global Carbon Atlas, www.globalcarbonatlas.org/en/$CO_2$-emissions

138    *Our Planet's $CO_2$ Home Page,* CO2.earth, www.co2. earth

Figure A.3 plots the level of GHG emissions per GDP, a commonly used metric of emissions intensity, across the same time span. It is useful when looking at the de-carbonisation of the national economy or energy system. If we look at economic measures like GDP and total GHG emissions, we can observe that although the $CO_2e$/million USD GDP followed similar decreasing patterns for all regions, with the world average dropping substantially, the European Union moved to first place and South Asia to the second in 2016.

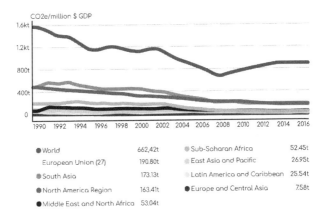

*Figure A.3: World GHG emissions per GDP and by geographical area from 1990 to 2016.*

Similar analysis can be done to better understand correlations between economic growth and environmental impacts, by showing specific GHGs (all of them measured by $CO_2$ equivalent) and GDP evolution by regions.

## CH$_4$ (methane)

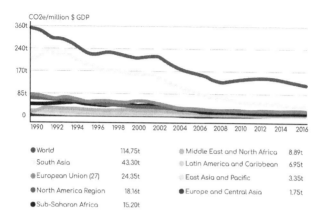

| | | | | |
|---|---|---|---|---|
| ● World | 114.75t | | ◉ Middle East and North Africa | 8.89t |
| South Asia | 43.30t | | ◌ Latin America and Caribbean | 6.95t |
| ◉ European Union (27) | 24.35t | | East Asia and Pacific | 3.35t |
| ● North America Region | 18.16t | | ● Europe and Central Asia | 1.75t |
| ● Sub-Saharan Africa | 15.20t | | | |

*Figure A.4: World CH$_4$ emissions per GDP and by geographical area from 1990 to 2016.*

Figure A.4 plots the decrease of $CO_2$e from methane ($CH_4$). Again, the World total shows a dramatic drop, but South Asia emissions remain the highest, followed by the European Union.

## F-gas (Fluorinated gases)

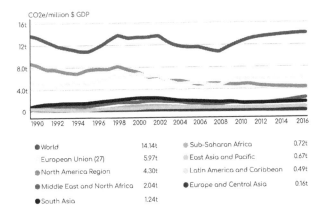

*Figure A.5: World F-gas emissions per GDP and by geographical area from 1990 to 2016.*

Figure A.5 plots the decrease of $CO_2e$ from fluorinated gases (F-gas). In 1990 the European Union emissions were much lower than those of the North American Region. Between 2000 and 2008 their emissions are roughly similar, but then the European Union emissions increase while North American emissions continue to decrease.

## NO₂ (Nitrogen Dioxide)

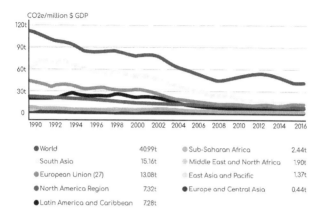

*Figure A.6: World NO₂ emissions per GDP and by geographical area from 1990 to 2016.*

Figure A.6 plots the decrease of CO₂e from Nitrogen Dioxide (NO₂). South Asia remains the highest contributor followed by the European union and the North American region. Sub-Saharan African had increases above the North American region between 1993 and 2006 before following a path similar to that of North America.

## CO$_2$ (Carbon Dioxide)

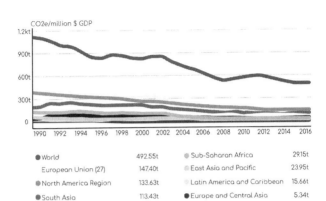

| | | | |
|---|---|---|---|
| ● World | 492.55t | ◉ Sub-Saharan Africa | 29.15t |
| European Union (27) | 147.40t | ◐ East Asia and Pacific | 23.95t |
| ◉ North America Region | 133.63t | ○ Latin America and Caribbean | 15.66t |
| ● South Asia | 113.43t | ● Europe and Central Asia | 5.34t |
| ● Middle East and North Africa | 41.20t | | |

*Figure A.7: World CO$_2$ emissions per GDP and by geographical area from 1990 to 2016.*

Figure A.7 plots the decrease of CO$_2$e from CO$_2$. The European Union and North America remain the highest contributors. Their emissions are similar with the European Union dipping below North America between 2006 and 2017, but then increasing again to be the highest contributor.

Another way to analyse the carbon-intensity of those regions is the correlation between economic growth as annual percentage and total GHG emissions.

The following graphs are a correlation between what is known as "energy intensity" (energy used per unit of service or value provided – in our graphs we replace "energy used" by "CO$_2$e") and "value provided" by "USF million GDP", which ends up in a more specific term, "carbon intensity", which is the measure of CO$_2$ produced per dollar of GDP. In other words, it's a measure of how much $CO_2$ we emit when we generate one dollar in our economy.[139]

The second variable, GDP annual growth, is shown only to reinforce the evidence about the trend of the whole economy. However, energy/GDP ratios are a very rough, aggregated, and sometimes misleading metric, because they combine changes in technical efficiency, human behaviour, and the composition of GDP.[140]

Figures A.8 to A.16 show the $CO_2$e/million USD GDP along the Y-Axis on the left and the GDP annual % growth along the Y-Axis on the right, from 1990 to 2019 along the X-Axis.

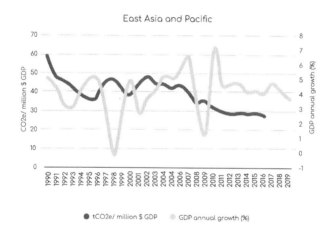

*Figure A.8: East Asia and Pacific $CO_2$ emissions per GDP and by annual growth from 1990 to 2019.*

139    *Global Historical Emissions*, Climate Watch Data, www.climatewatchdata.org/ghg-emissions?end_year=2016&regions=&start_year=1990

140    *World Development Indicators*, The World Bank Data, www.data.worldbank.org/indicator/NY.GDP.MKTP.KD.ZG

In Figure A.8 (East Asia and the Pacific), the total $CO_2e$ emissions per GDP fell gradually from 60 to approximately 25 in the period 1990 to 2017. GDP annual growth drops from 5% to just below 4% in that period, but there is a dramatic drop to 0% in 1998 and another drop to 1% in 2009. The highest growth of 7% corresponds with lower $CO_2e$ emissions in 2010, but this growth then drops back down to between 4 and 5% in the years following while the emissions remain stable.

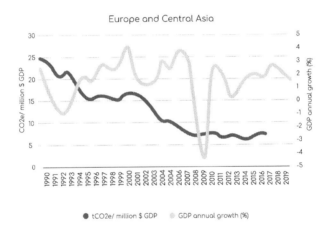

*Figure A.9: Europe and Central Asia $CO_2$ emissions per GDP and by annual growth from 1990 to 2019.*

In Figure A.9 (Europe and Central Asia), the total $CO_2e$ emissions per GDP fell fairly sharply from 25 to approximately 8 in the period 1990 to 2017. GDP annual growth drops from just above 2% to just above 1% in that period but remains fairly stable between 2% and 4% for much of the period. There is a drop to -1% in1992 and another dramatic drop to just above -5% in 2009 with highs of 4% in 1999 and 2006.

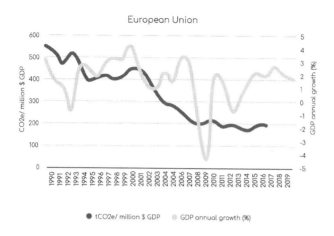

*Figure A.10: European Union $CO_2$ emissions per GDP and by annual growth from 1990 to 2019.*

In Figure A.10 (European Union), the total $CO_2$e emissions per GDP fell fairly sharply from 550 to 200 in the period 1990 to 2017. GDP annual growth drops from approximately 3.5% to just above 1% in that period but remains fairly stable between 1% and 3% for much of the period. There is a drop to just above -1% in1993 and another dramatic drop to just above -5% in 2009 with highs around 4% in 2000 and 2006. The shape of the graph is very similar to that in Figure A.9.

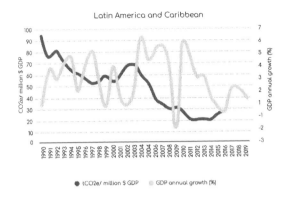

*Figure A.11: Latin America and Caribbean $CO_2$ emissions per GDP and by annual growth from 1990 to 2019.*

In Figure A.11 (Latin America and the Caribbean), the total $CO_2$e emissions per GDP fell fairly sharply from just above 90 to approximately 25 in the period 1990 to 2017. The GDP line for annual growth zigzags up and down during the period with the highs just above 6% in 2004 and 6% in 2010, and the lowest at -2% in 2009.

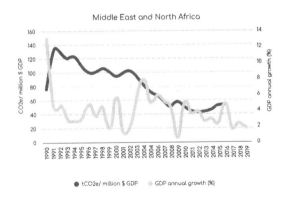

*Figure A.12: Middle East and North Africa $CO_2$ emissions per GDP and by annual growth from 1990 to 2019.*

In Figure A.12 (Middle East and North Africa), the pattern for total $CO_2e$ emissions per GDP and GDP annual growth are very different. The $CO_2e$ emissions initially rose from 80 to just under 140 in the period 1990 to 1991 before falling at a steady rate to about 50 2017. The GDP line for annual growth initially drops from 13% to 4% in the first year and then zigzags up and down regularly until 2019 when it is just below 2%. In 2001 and 2009 the GDP annual growth reached 1% and close to 0% respectively, with a high of 8% in2004.

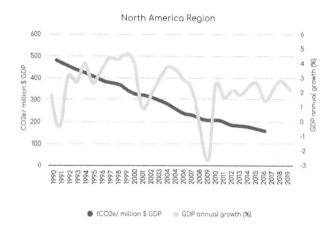

*Figure A.13: North America $CO_2$ emissions per GDP and by annual growth from 1990 to 2019.*

In Figure A.13 (North America), the total $CO_2e$ emissions per GDP fell fairly steadily, in almost a straight line, from 500 to approximately 150 in the period 1990 to 2017. GDP annual growth increases from just below 2% to just above 2% in that period with some increase above 3% from 1992 to 2007. There was an initial drop to just below 0% in 1991, another to 1% in 2001, and another to -3% in 2009.

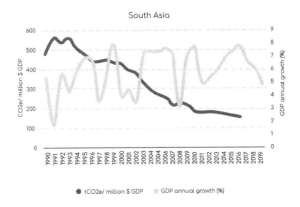

*Figure A.14: South Asia CO$_2$ emissions per GDP and by annual growth from 1990 to 2019.*

In Figure A.14 (South Asia), the total CO$_2$e emissions per GDP initially rose from just below 500 to just below 600 in the period 1990 to 1993. It then dropped steadily to approximately 150 in 2017. The GDP line for annual growth zigzags up and down during the period with several highs at 8% and several lows between 2 and 3 %.

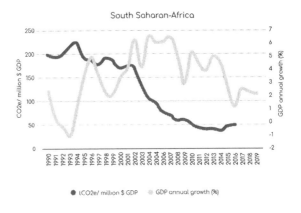

*Figure A.15: South Saharan-Africa CO₂ emissions per GDP and by annual growth from 1990 to 2019.*

In Figure A.15 (South Saharan-Africa), the total CO$_2$e emissions per GDP initially rose from 200 to 230 in the period 1990 to 1994. They then remained fairly stable until 2002 before dropping steadily to approximately 50 in 2017. The GDP line for annual growth initially drops from 2.5% in 1990 to -1% in 1993 before rising to 5% in1996. Following another drop to 2% in 199 it rose to nearly 7% before slowly decreasing back to 2% in 2019.

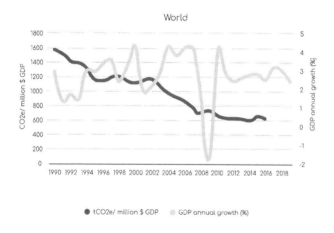

*Figure A.16: World CO₂ emissions per GDP and by annual growth from 1990 to 2019.*

In Figure A.16 (World), the total CO$_2$e emissions per GDP fell fairly sharply from 1600 to just over 600 in the period 1990 to 2017. GDP annual growth drops from approximately 3% to just above 2% in that period but remains fairly stable between 1.5% and 4.5% for much of the period. There is a dramatic drop to just above -2% in2009. The shape of the graph is very similar to that in Figures A.9 and A.10.

So there isn't a correlation at all? Which is good news because it means one can achieve one without the other. For developing countries and most importantly organisations within them it means they can grow without damaging Earth through their efforts. We live in a hyperconnected world so it's key that we all ensure, demand and help each one of our ecosystems towards achieving Sustainable, Happy Profit by design.

By looking at the following facts published by the US Environment Protection Agency (EPA) it's possible to look again at how $CO_2$ has mostly fueled GHG. Specifically, $CO_2$ contributes 65% of total GHG emissions. In addition, electricity generation (25%) and agriculture (24%) are the most relevant economic sectors leading to GHG emissions.

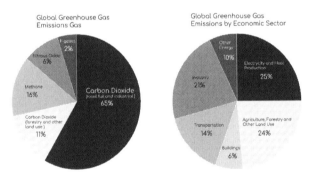

Source: IPCC (2014) based on global emissions from 2010. Details about the sources included in these estimates can be found in the Contribution of Working Group III to the Fifth Assessment Report of the Intergovernmental Panel on Climate Change.

*Figure A.17: Global GHG Emissions by Gas and Economic Sector based on data from IPCC (2014). Adapted from www. epa.gov[141]*

---

141    *Global Greenhouse Gas Emissions Data*, United States Environmental Protection Agency (EPA), www.epa.gov/ghgemissions/global-greenhouse-gas-emissions-data

Figure A.17 consists of two pie charts showing global greenhouse emissions by types of gas and economic sector. $CO_2$ from fossil fuels and industry accounts for 65% of gases while those from forestry and other land use account for just 11%. The three remaining gases, methane, nitrous oxide and F-gases account for 16%, 6% and 2% respectively. In terms of economic sectors, electricity and heat production produce 25% with a further 24% coming from agriculture, forestry and other land use. Industry contributes 21% and transportation 14%. The remainder come from buildings at 6% and a general "other" at 10%.

The WRI has developed some models to think about the consequences of not taking action on GHG emissions. Certainly, the Paris Agreement and SGDs are the framework of these models. If countries do not commit to these goals, worst scenarios will play out.

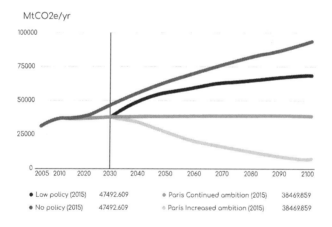

*Figure A.18: Total GHG Emissions data up to 2010 and projection paths by policies ambition from WRI[142]*

142     *WRI's Sustainability Data*, World Resources Institute (WRI), https://www.wri.org/sustainability-wri/dashboard

In figure A.18, GHG Emissions are shown in $CO_2e$/yr on the Y-Axis, from 0 to 100,000, with data and predictive data plotted from 2005 to 2100 on the X-Axis. Four graph lines represent possible scenarios in the cases of low policy, no policy, Paris's continued ambition and Paris's increased ambition. In 2030, the "low" and "no" policies predict emissions of approximately 70,000 Mt/yr. The line for no policy continues to rise steadily, ending at just below 95,000 Mt/yr by 2100. The low policy curves more slowly and reaches just below 75,000 Mt/yr the same date. The two Paris lines are at approximately 40,000 in 2300. The continued ambition line continues in a straight line while the increased ambition drops slowly to about 5,000 by 2100.

It's up to us at micro level to develop constant enhancements to go beyond regulations and support those agreements being regenerative by design so that in fact the best-case scenario does happen.

I'm certain we can make it. Are you part of the solution?

# SUSTAINABLE HAPPY PROFIT

HOW TO CREATE A SUSTAINABILITY FRAMEWORK THAT WORKS FOR YOU.

## INES GARCIA

HANDBOOK

I know we're used to operating by the maxim "you can have cheap, fast or good: pick two," but with the triad of sustainability, happiness and profit you really can have all three. In fact, with those things as a focus they actually nourish each other, therefore are more rewarding.

The figures speak for themselves, we can't continue in the spiral of self-destruction which our organisations are operating in today. [1] There is a better way.

Companies are composed of individuals and we can do both; do good and do well. I'm not pretending this is a walk in the park; it's not a matter of simply dictating instructions, it requires conscious effort from all individuals.

The whole is greater than the sum of its parts:

- You can have great sustainability practices but without the talent and profit, it won't endure.

- You can have a happy workforce but if you're unaware of your practices and making no money, it won't last.

- You can make a profit but if you do not have a creative driving force, energy and materials for it, it won't sustain.

The three are interrelated.

In the book **Sustainable Happy Profit** [2], I've used broad brush strokes to paint a wide picture of what a sustainable, happy and profitable business is. Brought it to life with real-life examples and stories, on how to move from theory to practice.

From energy companies which switch 80% fossil fuel to 80% renewables, and in doing so increase their profits by 28%, to health care services which move from 4 employees to 10,000 in 8 years.

Imagine a world where every employee is a problem-solver with the mantra of continuous improvement. Amongst these examples there are many more industries', teams' and individuals' stories so that you can see how to cross the chasm between theoretical agreement and rolling up your sleeves to just get on with it.

We have no time to lose.

Since the beginning of 2020, much has come more apparent.

- Food insecurity: 135 million people in 55 countries face acute hunger.

- Climate crisis: daily global carbon dioxide ($CO_2$) emissions in early April 2020 were 17% lower than average daily emissions in 2019

- Force for good: globally we have turned to help others and fight for what matters.

Depending on your current business model or as a Small and Medium-sized Enterprises (SME) it can be tricky to pick out what is doable for you. Maybe you don't have much say over the premises you use, or you work remotely. Maybe you don't have the capital to invest in large-scale changes. Maybe you provide a niche product or service which can't easily be altered. This handbook is for you.

The aim of this handbook is to pull together advice and suggestions to help all businesses make immediate changes, while acknowledging that some things are currently simply impossible and may first need a new lens applied for some. And that's OK. Something is better than nothing. Do what you can.

In this handbook we'll focus on the 'sustainable' part of **Sustainable Happy Profit** because, it's not just the most pressing challenge that humanity has faced to date, it is also a myth that it requires compromise. We need to embrace this paradigm shift so that we can thrive in balance in the biosphere.

In my experience, it's also the area that smaller organisations find most daunting but also therefore the most satisfying to address. Not to mention that success here has a knock-on effect on happiness and profit too, which is what we're here for, right?

We'll start by looking at things which an organisation with even only one employee can do and work our way up from there.

# A Simple Frame

As part of **Sustainable Happy Profit** we talked about making your own framework. When you are doing so, remind yourself that it's really easy to make things complex, anyone can do that!

On my own journey I discovered how quickly the overload of information comes. Reflecting on this, I ended up structuring my efforts with three key areas of focus:

*Figure 1: People, Product, Planet pillars.*

It serves as a simple frame to measure and monitor performance as well as aligning improvements. The three items act as the pillars of the ecosystem I am building towards.

To get into more concrete territory I formed a matrix from four variables for each of the pillars:

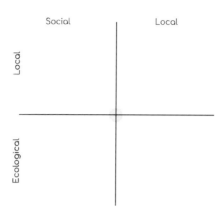

*Figure 2: Social-Ecological-Global-Local matrix.*

I came across these four lenses, Global, Local, Social and Ecological, from Kate Raworth's work, presented as a holistic approach upon the launch of the Amsterdam City Doughnut. [3]

For example, under People (Local & Social quadrant) you may want to invest in quality education to increase opportunities in your area, from employees' percentage of time allocated to volunteer initiatives helping to build tomorrow's workforce. Under Products (Global & Ecological), could be included reduction of physically released (materiality). An example is the Better Estimates short book which I only made available digitally. Under Planet (Ecological & Global), the percentage of Year-on-Year business travel could be reduced. The biggest impact, either locally or globally, will depend on your current operations and context.

And that's my frame; that's it. Simple. So that one can easily categorise, measure and monitor each area (People, Product,

Planet) on the continuous improvement journey of **Sustainable Happy Profit**.

Feel free to use it, to enhance it or to make your own!

The three most pressing areas that any organisation of any size must get on with now:

1. System Map
2. Carbon Footprint
3. Waste Slash

# #1 System Map

A system map is a powerful technique for any organisation. It illustrates how value flows from inception or order through to its delivery and use.

When organising and optimising our to-dos we often look vertically at the process; how a department can be leaner or how a step in the delivery process can be streamlined. Sometimes we get so tangled in the details we forget to look at the whole, where the customer is at one end with your product delivered at the other end. Try depicting the current state of affairs by connecting the sections horizontally as shown in Figure 3.

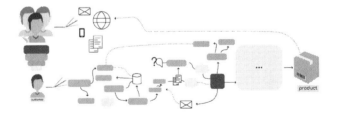

*Figure 3: example of a partial systems process System Map.*

Figure 3 shows different processes, depicted by various symbols, and how they connect with each other, moving from the customer's order to the final product. At various points in the process there may be a problem, a manual step, multiple communication and systems involved... Perhaps one process is waiting too long for other processes or parts before it can move on to the next stage in the process. Each of these represent opportunities to assess and streamline the production process and remove waste from the system.

Doing this makes work visible, gives context and enables alignment. I explore this in much more depth in Part One of **Sustainable Happy Profit** [2].

Draw it! How does your System Map look today? That is how you *anchor*, so that you can identify and deepen your understanding of how the value creation flows through your system so that you can then make it better.

There are three tools that can help you to deepen your System Map:

**Competing Values Framework [4]**

Research from Quinn and Rohrbaugh showed that you can use a set of questions to locate your current place on each quadrant in the framework (see Figure 4), which represents a way of being, seeing, managing, and organising.

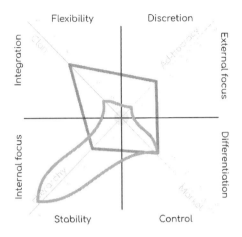

*Figure 4: Competing Values Framework example,*
*a kite on a matrix.*

You will end up with something looking like a kite on a matrix, as there will be one quadrant more dominant than the other three, this allows you to diagnose your organisation's current and desired cultures. Doing this across multiple teams brings awareness and a common language. It highlights commonalities and discrepancies, identifies trends, finds areas of synergy and detects resistance. For example, the value of allowing employee flexibility to boost creativity may compete with the need to keep customers satisfied with the products or services provided. A desire to create and innovate may conflict with the need for incremental change that allows for analysis, testing and redesign. It is important to create a work environment that allows for the integration of employee goals and the company's overall objectives. Try it!

## SASB Materiality Map® [5]

Identifies the sustainability likelihood of issues by industry. You are presented with multiple dimensions and definitions. It's interactive so that you can drill down to further understand the financial and operational effects for your industry.

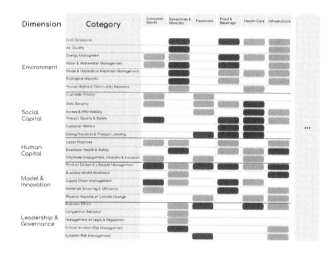

*Figure 5: Industry and dimensions matrix. Adapted from SASB Materiality Map®.*

In Figure 5, the columns contain aspects of production such as consumer goods, extractives and minerals processing, financials and health care, while the rows list general issues under dimensions such as environment, social capital and human capital. Each square is the colour coded based on how likely it is to be material for industries in that sector.

It will surface items such as the environmental impact of packing or physical risk due to an increased frequency and intensity of extreme weather events, emissions limiting regulations, etc it will focus the spectrum further within your context.

## Social-Ecological Impact Assessment Tool [6]

A tool generated by Adolfo Chautón Pérez and the ENSO team (Figure 6) combines concepts from Doughnuts Economics, Theory of Change and SDGs, so that you can map your context and specific Sustainable Development Goals with fields of impact, scopes, actions and results.

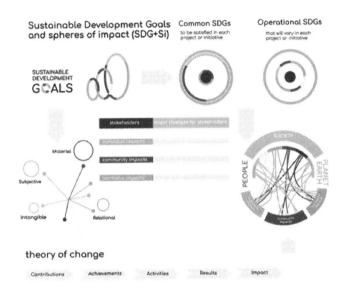

*Figure 6: Industry and dimensions matrix. Adapted from DEAL.*

In the top left of the map are sustainable development goals and spheres of impact (SDG+Si). Below these are sustainability goals with an arrow to the right points towards the selected common SDGs for an organisation that must be satisfied and also specific operational SDGs that will vary between different projects or initiatives. From the sustainability goals there is another arrow pointing down towards a mind map composed of four variables: material, relational, intangible and subjective. From there leads to the theory of change to measure efforts from contributions all the way to impact. Above this is a table with four rows representing stakeholders and individual, community and territorial impacts. On the right of the diagram, below the common SDGs and operational SDGs, is an arrow pointing to a web diagram where it all comes together. This shows this interconnectivity between people, society and planet earth, as well as individual, community and territorial impacts.

Now pause. Out of these three enhancements to your System Map, plot in your frame (People, Product, Planet / Social-Ecological-Local-Global) the top items to be addressed.

# #2 Carbon Footprint

Your immediate priority is to reduce carbon emissions to zero and to stabilise the global temperatures as low as we possibly can. The aim is to cut carbon emissions 'at source' as much as possible, right now.

Your target is to reduce at least your current carbon emission by 50% per year from now on, and aim to be fossil fuel free by 2030, at individual level and organisational level.

Every organisation, from sole traders to multinational corporations, can measure and audit. Armed with that information you can start to take steps.

There are four main variables to focus on here:

1. Energy
2. Transport
3. Physical
4. Digital

Use your System Map to spot the end-to-end value chain, highlighted horizontally with which variable is most present in each step of the way.

Emissions go beyond your daily site operations. In the following table you can find what each variable is comprised of (*assess*), your immediate step from today (*action*) and improvement measures for your tracker (*account*):

| | Assess ? | Action ✓ | Account |
|---|---|---|---|
| **Energy** | That is from either building space and/or wherever individuals work from, electricity, heating, cooling etc | Your action today is to switch to 100% run on renewable energy 24/7, site, personal, suppliers, all employees | Add on your tracker the current consumption and set energy efficiency targets from now on, such as reduction of energy consumption by 25%.<br>- any new bulb replacement to energy efficient<br>- use natural light<br>- switch lights and devices off any time not in use<br>- smart controls; thermostat, water, power outlets<br>- solar energy use and capture |
| **Transport** | That is all forms that move (to and from) people and product. From flights, cars, vans, buses, rail … | Your action today is to switch to 100% renewable energy for all transport, wherever people and product may be coming and going. | Add on your tracker the current transportation and set reduction targets from now on, such as:<br>- 75% less air travel from 2019 levels and<br>- a 50% reduction on any travel emissions year-on-year and<br>- offsetting 100% remaining.<br>- also reduce fleet use including delivery frequency and route planning. |
| **Physical** | That is all forms of materials that you use, from the products, to packaging, wrapping for pallets, the source of the materials, optimise the use of building space in all operations. | Your action today is to switch to 75% recycled and reclaimed materials for new products.<br>Create a feasible process to recuperate at least 50% of your products at the end of life.<br>Increase your digital offerings over physical. | Add on your tracker the current materials used, where do they come from, footprint on transport and manufacturing, process to recuperate them back into the value chain,<br>- include reduction volume of paper and printing, mailing and materials and other business as usual activities.<br>- any further purchases of equipment and materials from second hand or reclaimed<br>- 100% green cleaning products and practices |
| **Digital** | That is all forms of devices, applications, programs, servers etc your whole organisation uses today. *"The internet consumes a lot of electricity. 416.2TWh per year to be precise. To give you some perspective, that's more than the entire United Kingdom."* [17] | Your action today is to switch to at least 50% renewable energy for digital technology; applications and solutions. | Add on your tracker all your applications, from email client to project management tool or design software application, find out the use and emissions set targets of 25% reduction year-on-year. |

The four variables (energy, transport, physical and digital) are also to be applied across your supply chain. That's emissions caused in producing other inputs your business relies on, and in using any products you create for others. Take an inventory of your suppliers and partners, facilitate a conversation about where you all stand and your urge that you all align in your efforts. Advocacy and setting clear goals across your supply chain is key. We're most effective when we work together. Get a clear commitment to tangible, measurable actions and work with vendors towards total reductions of 25-50% emissions in the next 5 years. Working together towards this common goal, you may need to apply the concept of autotomy (covered in **Sustainable Happy Profit**) if there is no interest nor progress within six months.

Reducing emissions and ending fossil fuels use does also substantially reduce air pollution and slow down ocean acidification whilst reducing pressure on biodiversity. This is the one initiative that has positive repercussions to three other planetary boundaries. [8]

Yet, reducing emissions is not enough, we must draw back the carbon that has already been released to the biosphere. **Become a carbon sink.** There is one way to do so, and that's planting more trees.

Looking at your frame of People, Planet, Product; what feasible areas do you have to invite nature back in? Where are spaces in which you can plant more trees? Which areas can you influence and support to plant more trees? How can you restore the land in areas that you operate?

Just planting more trees is not enough either, we need a global effort to protect the current land, avoid further disasters such as wildfires and reinstate autochthonous biodiversity. Nature's model has worked for most of the planet's history, so let's be inspired by that as we plan our improvements and innovations. [9]

Quick recap 4 key areas to decarbonise:

- Energy efficiency, less use per unit vs now
- Low carbon electricity, green switch
- Shift away from fossil fuels, now
- Carbon sink, to restore balance

Time for a pause. Out of these enhancements to your System Map, plot the top item to address in your frame:

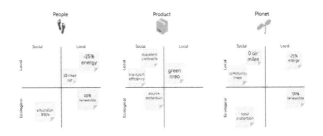

*Figure 7: Sample Social-Ecological-Global-Local matrix under each People-Product-Planet pillars frame.*

In Figure 7, the Local, Global, Social and Ecological quadrants are plotted out under the headings, "People", "Product" and "Planet". Under "People", the Local-Ecological quadrant has as an example an initiative to plant 20 trees per person and a reduction of 25% of current energy use. In the Global-Social quadrant we have efforts on education in line with the SDGs, and in the Global-Ecological quadrant shows "100% renewable" from switch of suppliers. This is repeated under each heading and provides a visual way in which to analyse priorities towards your sustainability goals.

The first step in any process is an assessment of where you are. How will you know if you've made progress if you don't know where you started? The good news about measurement is that there's lots of help out there. One person just needs to take the initiative; doable in any organisation. B Corporation provides a "free, open-source, filterable, downloadable, curated library of tools to help businesses take climate action" [10]. [11] This functions as a one-stop-shop for resources and really does have something for every organisation to enable them to take the very first steps.

If you don't have the time or the confidence to audit yourself, you can outsource to a professional. In the UK, Ofgem (the organisation which regulates gas and electricity companies) provides advice, information and links to grants and services which can support your business in becoming more energy efficient. [12]

If you already have some goals in mind it can be useful to consider them from a fresh perspective. Sometimes we set goals because they 'feel' right or because it seems like what everyone is doing. Actually, it's important that our goals are in the right place for us. We have to consider what we're trying to achieve when changing anything; one thing we should definitely be aiming for is resilience. If the last couple of years have shown us anything it's that we must be flexible and prepared for the unexpected. Assessing our goals against resilience criteria is a helpful way to check whether they are useful and all-encompassing.

# #3 Waste Slash

The third pressing area for any organisation is waste, and it's highly interrelated with the previous two. The value of a company's goods and services is relative to the waste it generates. Sustainability and happiness are not at the expense of profit but a means to it.

There is a flaw in our current design system; we have organised ourselves in an imagined process without a means to recover materials used. It's often referred to as a 'take-make-waste' model, a linear economy.

Imagine a world without waste, leaving us with nothing to throw away. We must redefine our faulty linear system as a circular one, so that those can reenter the marketplace. What's called a circular economy.

There are three areas that can help you to slash your waste:

**Real Estate**

You want to run on clean energy, with an immediate switch to 100% renewable energy 24/7, including your site, your suppliers, your employees and onwards beyond your virtual organisation boundaries.

Now, switching is easy. The question is how can we collect perishable natural energy? Especially solar. "If humanity could capture one tenth of one percent of the solar energy striking the earth – one part in one thousand - we would have access to six times as much energy as we consume in all forms today, with almost no greenhouse gas emissions."[13]

Look at distributed generation by solar power, you can reduce energy costs by 45-60% look at available spaces you may have for this and also note there are grants and financing support for such efforts often available.

If you do have any real estate and or temporary rented space, think about kicking off a program focused on the sustainability of it. Look at all angles, from aligning with LEED Platinum v4 standards, to the pursuit of Net Zero Carbon certification on your facilities, space usage and energy reduction efforts, how to embed a blackwater recycling system, etc.

Start a lamp replacement program, if you change old lamps you might have 60-70% of energy savings·

Did you know that AC can double your bills? Favour natural breeze or fans over AC. Even heating costs increase by 8% over each extra 10C. Did you know that turning the thermostat right up doesn't heat the room any quicker?

In terms of water efficiency, if you implement digital controls and automatic solenoid valves you can reduce water consumption. Elevated tanks simplify the plumbing system and you can use a water catchment from storm drain systems.

For example, with simple controls Banco Do Brazil estimated a 17.9% reduction of its water consumption in 2019.

Either building space or individuals' workspace can be adapted, by utilising doors, windows and smarter office layout to take advantage of natural ventilation and light and reduce costs by around 30%.

You may already have an inventory of assets. Ensure that you have their lifespan there, each line is an opportunity to make the replacement a better product and better for the people, planet, and profit.

**Value Stream Mapping [14]**

It's a common exercise in the Agile arena to surface any potential improvement in our day-to-day processes. It comes from the lean manufacturing revolution that makes things visible by embedding materials and information on flow diagramming to introduce lean practices.

The idea is to bring together representatives of each vertical section of your System Map and collaborate to outline time spent in between each vertical area (think of it being in a queue ready to be consumed by the next vertical step), where you co-create ways to streamline it.

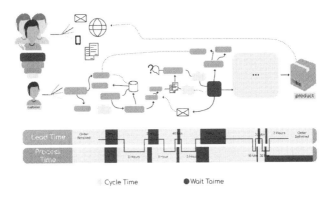

*Figure 8: example of extending a System Map with lead and process time.*

In Figure 8, the relationship between lead time and process time is shown. The top part of the diagram is a diagram of the process. As mentioned earlier on the left is an image representing the customer and on the right is the final product. In between are all the processes required to create the product. There is an additional line looping back to the world, sales and prospective customers. Below this are two bars, one showing lead time and the other process time. This outlined the time spent working on parts of the product development, design and production, and waiting times in between each of these steps. For example, an order is received but it is three hours before the first part of the process begins. This process may take three hours, followed by a three hour wait time which incurs a delay before the next step in the process. Figure 8 shows eight periods of lead time, or delay between the six periods of process time. The aim of lean manufacturing is to minimise these wait times in order to shorten the overall time needed between the order being received and delivered.

You may have already started! Pick up your System Map. I'd highly recommend investing in an experienced professional to facilitate this exercise.

### Scientific Method

We cover this idea in extent in the last chapter of **Sustainable Happy Profit** [2], in the area of *bets*. For the content so far your organisation most likely has tons of ideas on how to improve the people, product and planet. We know not all ideas will succeed, so you want to maximise the returns from your efforts.

Hypotheses are the initial building blocks for the scientific method. Make an 'educated guess' based on prior knowledge and observation, to which you can design experiments. Refine according to your results.

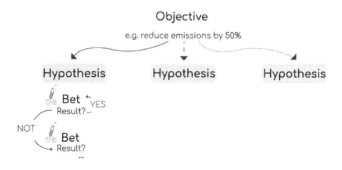

*Figure 9: example of a Scientific Method structure.*

213

Figure 9 shows the objective of reducing emissions by 50%. Three possible hypotheses flow from the objective. A 'bet' or best guest is made from the strongest hypothesis; if the result is positive, then the bet can be developed further, but if it is negative, then a new bet is made and trialled.

Use this process to experiment within prespecified boundaries of effort and time, so that you can decide whether to pivot or persevere. Therefore minimising risk and waste.

---

Don't do it alone, the whole is greater than the sum of its parts.

We explored in Part Two of **Sustainable Happy Profit** [2] why it's so important to have happiness to thrive—apart from it just being a good, human trait to care about the well-being of others—and how this in turn helps to maximise profits in a big sustainable circle.

The Woohoo inc. survey found that the single factor which has the biggest impact on an individual's happiness is whether they were able to say "I did work that I knew was meaningful and made a positive difference for someone else". [15] What more meaningful and positive difference is there than to contribute to a thriving planet, people and products? Yes, there is more to happiness than this, in **Sustainable Happy Profit** we cover much more on the subject. In this handbook we are focusing on how to create a sustainability framework that works for you. So capitalise on this and make sustainability a collaborative effort. Ask your *people* where they think there are improvements to be made—they know the intricacies of their daily work life better than you do and may have some ideas you would never have come up with. That goes beyond employees per se, look at your System Map. They may even already be unilaterally doing wonderful things which could be disseminated wider, if only you knew about them. [16]

Hopefully this handbook has provided you with a host of ideas, not just to think about, but to build on what you already have.

There seems little more to say other than, 'Onwards'. Let's see what changes and improvements we can make together.

See you on the other side.

*www.SustainableHappyProfit.com*

[1] Sustainable Development Goals, *E-Handbook on SDG Indicators*, UN Statistics Wiki, https://unstats.un.org/wiki/display/SDGeHandbook/Home

[2] Ines Garcia, *Sustainable Happy Profit,* (Get Agile Ltd, 2021)

[3] Exploring Doughnut Economics, *Introducing the Amsterdam City Doughnut*, www.kateraworth.com/2020/04/08/amsterdam-city-doughnut

[4] The Competing Values Culture Assessment, by Kim S. Cameron

Robert E. Quinn, www.boomhogeronderwijs.nl/media/8/download_pdf_culture_assessment_workbook.pdf

[5] SASB's Materiality Map®, https://materiality.sasb.org

[6] Doughnut Economics Action Lab, *Social-Ecological Impact Assessment Tool*, https://doughnuteconomics.org/tools-and-stories/98?users_page=2

[7] Website Carbon, *How is your website impacting the planet?* www.websitecarbon.com/

[8] *Planetary boundaries,* Wikipedia, https://en.wikipedia.org/wiki/Planetary_boundaries

[9] *Ask Nature*, Biomimicry Institute, www.asknature.org

[10] *B Corporation*, Twitter, https://twitter.com/BCorporation/status/1385291334353838080

[11] B Climate Tools Base, B Corp Climate Collective, www.bcorpclimatecollective.org/tools

[12] *Find business energy efficiency grants and schemes*, ofgem, https://www.ofgem.gov.uk/information-consumers/energy-

advice-businesses/find-business-energy-efficiency-grants-and-schemes

[13] Scientific American, *Smaller, cheaper, faster: Does Moore's law apply to solar cells?* https://blogs.scientificamerican.com/guest-blog/smaller-cheaper-faster-does-moores-law-apply-to-solar-cells

[14] Agile Alliance, Value Stream Mapping www.agilealliance.org/resources/experience-reports/value-stream-mapping-how-to-see-where-youre-going-by-seeing-where-you-are

[15] *Our Study of Good Days at Work*, Woohoo Inc, www.woohooinc.com/happiness-at-work/study-good-work-days

[16] Julie Rains, *7 Business Lessons From Undercover Boss, American Express*, https://www.americanexpress.com/en-us/business/trends-and-insights/articles/7-business-lessons-from-undercover-boss/

# FREE DOWNLOAD

No more finger in
the air
*guesstimates*.

Printed in Great Britain
by Amazon

11493360R00125